DRED AND HARRIET SCOTT

DRED AND HARRIET SCOTT

A Family's Struggle for Freedom

Gwenyth Swain

BOREALIS BOOKS

Borealis Books is an imprint of the Minnesota Historical Society Press.
www.borealisbooks.org

www.mnhs.org/mhspress

The Minnesota Historical Society Press is a member of the Association of American
University Presses.

Manufactured in the United States of America

10 9 8 7 6 5 4 3 2 1

♾ The paper used in this publication meets the minimum requirements of the
American National Standard for Information Sciences–Permanence for Printed Library
Materials, ANSI Z39.48–1984.

International Standard Book Number 0-87351-482-3 (cloth)
0-87351-483-1 (paper)

Library of Congress Cataloging-in-Publication Data
Swain, Gwenyth, 1961–
Dred and Harriet Scott : a family's struggle for freedom / Gwenyth Swain.
p. cm.
Includes bibliographical references and index.
Contents: Dred and the Blow boys – Big changes – Meeting Harriet –
Young and likely – Freedom lost and found and lost again –
The Dred Scott decision – Free at last.
ISBN 0-87351-482-3 (hardcover : alk. paper) –
ISBN 0-87351-483-1 (pbk. : alk. paper)
1. Scott, Dred, 1809–1858–Juvenile literature. 2. Scott, Harriet, d. ca. 1870–
Juvenile literature. 3. Slaves–United States–Biography–Juvenile literature.
4. Scott, Dred,1809–1858–Trials, litigation, etc.–Juvenile literature. 5. Slaves–
Legal status, laws, etc.–United States–Juvenile literature. 6. Slavery–
Law and legislation–United States–Juvenile literature.
[1. Scott, Dred, 1809–1858. 2. Scott, Harriet, d. ca. 1870. 3. Slavery–
Law and legislation. 4. African Americans–Biography.] I. Title.
E444.S38S93 2004
973.7′115′0922–dc22
2003019909

TABLE OF CONTENTS

⚜ ACKNOWLEDGMENTS ⚜

THE AUTHOR WISHES TO ACKNOWLEDGE THE CON-
tributions of many individuals and organizations to this book.

For their helpful comments on the manuscript in progress and for generous sharing of expertise, I thank the following individuals: Daniel S. Dupre; Walter Ehrlich; Mary Jane McDaniel; Marcia Marshall; Bob Moore, Jefferson National Expansion Memorial; Thomas Shaw, Historic Fort Snelling; and Shannon M. Pennefeather.

For research assistance, I acknowledge the following people and places: Karen Blackwell; Alice Scott Burris; Thomas Carney, *Old Huntsville Magazine*; Wayne Cosby, Southampton, Virginia, Circuit Court; Thomas Dewey, Jefferson National Expansion Memorial; Sherry Falter; Noel Holobeck, St. Louis Public Library; Thomas Kenny; Office of the Judge of Probate, Huntsville, Alabama; Ranee Pruitt, Huntsville–Madison County Public Library Archives; the reference staffs of the Minnesota, Missouri, and Wisconsin state historical societies; Darrell A. Russel; and Joyce Williams and Minneola Dixon, Oakwood College Archives.

For their support of this project from its inception, particular thanks go to the staff of Borealis Books and to Debbie Miller.

And many thanks to my sister Christanne Traxler and to my very patient husband, Vince Dolan.

DRED AND HARRIET SCOTT

CHILDREN ARE PRECIOUS. EVERY PARENT KNOWS that. Yet slaves in America were never really free to hold onto their children. They couldn't keep their babies close to them. Slave babies belonged not to their parents, but to Master.

When a slave mother went to work in the fields at harvest-time, when all hands were needed, she laid her baby down under a tree or under a bush alongside the field. She hoped the shade held until noontime. That's when she would be allowed to hold and feed and comfort her baby again.

When a slave father drove his master's carriage into town, he worried about the young child he left behind at the master's big house. He hoped the child wouldn't get into trouble. Elderly slaves often looked after the youngest slave children, but boys and girls as young as four or five were put to work. They ran errands, took water to other slaves working in the fields, or helped look after younger children.

It's likely that Dred Scott's first job was looking after a baby. A white baby, the son of his master. Fan the flies away from him. Keep him from crying. Watch for when he wets his diaper. All these things a slave boy of four or five could do.

Years later Dred asked for help from "them boys he was raised with," the Blow boys, sons of his master, Peter Blow. He asked them to help him fight for his freedom—and for the freedom of his wife, Harriet, and their children, Eliza and Lizzie.

That fight has a name: the Dred Scott Decision. The U.S. Supreme Court in Washington, D.C., made the decision about Dred's freedom in 1857. The verdict divided this country. Many think it helped to bring about a bloody, bloody war between the southern and the northern states.

Historians say the Court's decision was all about states' rights, citizenship rights, and a host of other big and important ideas. But to Dred Scott and Harriet Robinson Scott, it was simple. It was about children. It was about how precious their daughters were to them. It was about a dream Dred and Harriet had.

They dreamed that their children—the daughters of slaves— would live free.

CHAPTER ONE

Dred and the Blow Boys

BLOWS HAD BEEN IMPORTANT, WEALTHY PLANTERS in Virginia since the 1600s. Southampton County had been their home since long before the Revolutionary War. And the Olde Place had been a Blow family plantation for years before Dred Scott came to live there sometime in the early 1800s.

Dred may first have been a slave in Mary Scott's family. Mary was a white Virginia woman who married one of the Blows–Richard–in 1774. Life in Virginia in those days was hard, even for wealthy whites. The land around the Olde Place was swampy, and lots of people became sick and died. Mary was dead by 1781. Just about the only thing she left behind was a son, Peter Blow. Maybe somebody in Mary's family gave that boy Peter some slaves and one of those slaves had a baby named Dred. The first anyone heard of a slave named Dred Scott, he belonged to Peter Blow.

Dred was a fairly common name among Virginia slave boys. *Scott* was the last name of many whites in the area–and of some free blacks. But Dred Scott didn't go by two names then. No slave did. Slave owners didn't want slaves thinking they were like free blacks. So Dred was just plain *Dred,* or *Boy,* depending on the mood of his master.

Dred's master, Peter, was one of the least important and least

TOWER HILL.

Tower Hill was a Blow family plantation near the Olde Place,
where Dred most likely grew up.

wealthy of the Blows of Southampton County. But that didn't
mean he was unimportant or poor. He owned 860 acres along
the Gum Branch of the Nottoway River. His land wasn't too far
downstream from Tower Hill. That grand plantation was home to
the most powerful and wealthy Blows in that corner of Virginia.
At Tower Hill there were "broad fields alive with slaves [and]
spreading lawns shaded by lofty trees."

Even though running a plantation was a lot of work, Blow
men still found time to go deer hunting in the morning and
squirrel hunting in the afternoon. Blow slaves carried their hunting bags and guns through dense forests of hickory, oak, and
cypress. After the hunt, Blow women joined the men for mint
juleps. Blow slaves grew the mint in kitchen gardens, drew cool
water from deep wells, and served their masters and mistresses.

Come evening, carriages driven by other slaves brought the area's most important people to Tower Hill for hours of good food, good tobacco, and good conversation.

Perhaps at one of those gatherings, Peter Blow met a local girl named Elizabeth Taylor. The two married just before Christmas in 1800. Young Blows had always been cared for by blacks, so it was natural that Peter and Elizabeth would have a young slave like Dred care for their children. Dred may have been a play-mate for Thomas Vaughan, the Blows' first son, born in 1804. And he may have helped change diapers for the sickly twin boys, Richard Benjamin and William Taylor. They were born in 1808, when Dred was about five.

Even at that young age, it must have been clear that Dred wasn't going to grow to be very big. Not as big as the field hands who sold for five hundred dollars or more on the auction block. Dred was small and slight, his skin dark black. His ancestors were slaves from Africa. That set Dred apart from the lighter-skinned slaves at the Olde Place and Tower Hill. Their mothers were slaves and their fathers Blow men, although you never heard much said about it.

Blow masters made sure their slaves had food and shelter. They didn't want their human property to be damaged or too sickly to work. While caring for the Blow boys, Dred likely slept in their room—but on the floor, not on a bed. He probably also lived in a slave cabin on the grounds of the Olde Place. Such cabins had mud floors and thatched roofs that kept out some, but not all, of the rain. Beds were made of straw and stray bits of cotton, packed together in a sack-like mattress and set on pieces of wood near the ground. Until Dred was old enough to work in the fields, his only clothing was a shift—a rough cotton or flax shirt that reached to his knees.

Dred may have been a healthy boy or he may have been sickly. No one knows now. But he was surely healthier than the Blow boys. Those boys didn't last long. Thomas was dead by 1812, and Richard by 1813. William didn't last out his first year. The Blow girls fared better. Mary Anne, the oldest, seemed healthy. So did Elizabeth Rebecca, born in 1806, Charlotte Taylor, born in 1810, and Patsey, born in 1812.

But losing all those boys must have been hard on Peter and Elizabeth Blow. It must have been hard on Dred, too. In spite of being the boys' slave, he was also their friend and protector. Dred's master started looking around for a healthier place to live. He hoped to find a place where his children wouldn't sicken and waste away. And he hoped to find a place that might be healthier for his fortunes.

For Peter Blow wasn't prospering as a farmer in Virginia. The land he owned was worn out. Generations of Blows had farmed it before him. Peter owned twelve slaves, but several of them were children, like Dred. Others, such as old Solomon and a grown woman, Hannah, were house slaves. They did the cleaning, cooking, and other work in the big house. They weren't strong field hands, the kind of slaves who could bring in a good crop even from farmed-out land.

In 1814, Dred's master had a son, Peter, who seemed healthier than the ones who had died. Another son, Henry Taylor, was born in 1817. Dred may still have cared for the boys, but as a teenager he likely worked in the fields, trying to help his master make a profit growing crops in tired-out dirt. Master Blow needed all the workers he could get. But he still didn't have much luck as a farmer. He borrowed money again and again just to keep the land.

His older brother—a bachelor with no children—died, but he left Peter nothing. Instead, he gave land and money to two slaves and to a mixed-race girl who might have been his daughter. The Blows prided themselves on treating their slaves well. They believed that blacks were inferior to whites, but they also figured there was no reason to make slaves feel bad about it. For example, Blows didn't call house slaves *slaves*. They called them *servants*. Still, it must have been a shock to Peter Blow when his brother left money and land he could well have used to a couple of slaves and a mixed-race girl.

By 1818, Peter Blow was tired of trying to coax a living out of the land around the Olde Place. He had heard story after story of fortunes made growing cotton in the southwest. Everyone was talking about Alabama's cotton country. A Virginian who'd moved to Huntsville the year before wrote home that "there has not been a single instance of any person settling in this country who has . . . not become wealthy in a few years." Peter Blow was ready to be wealthy for a change.

He packed up his family—his wife, Elizabeth, the four girls, and the two young boys. They would ride on horseback or sit in wagons. Dred and the other slaves would walk the hundreds of miles to Huntsville where their master had already bought 160 acres of land. One slave who made the same trip remembered later, "Every time we look back and think 'bout home it make us sad." If Peter Blow worried that his slaves might try to run back home, he probably made them walk with their ankles or necks chained together. That's how countless slaves walked—over mountains, through streams, and across wilderness. Probably none of them would ever return home again. It was, as one man put it, a "returnless distance."

Dred probably helped keep the younger Blow children from wandering off the long trail to Alabama. Each night, he no doubt gathered sticks for the fire and set up tents for the Blows to sleep in. The slaves slept in the open air on piles of leaves or under one of Peter Blow's wagons.

While Peter Blow slept snug in his tent, his dreams were full of hope. He had heard tales of land so rich you hardly had to work it to make crops grow. Of cotton fetching twenty-five cents a pound. Of a healthy climate, a place free from the kinds of sicknesses that killed young boys.

House slaves like old Solomon and Hannah would have heard conversations between the master and the mistress. They may have heard reports of Alabama's cotton fields. "They are astonishingly large," one woman wrote, "from four to five hundred acres in a field!—It is without a parallel!" Such words thrilled the Blows. But to their slaves, those words meant not wealth but work. Backbreaking work.

DRED AND THE BLOW BOYS

Work on an established plantation like the Olde Place was hard enough. But when slaves moved to the frontier, no cabins would be waiting for them. There would be no kitchen garden planted with herbs and vegetables. There wouldn't even be a kitchen. Slaves would keep on sleeping under wagons until they could take a break from clearing and planting fields and harvesting crops. Then, they might have time to build rough lean-tos and cabins.

Dred was about fifteen when he moved with the Blows to Alabama. They had taken advantage of winter, when rugged frontier roads would be less muddy than usual. It's likely they arrived at their new home around Christmas 1818. Dred and the other slaves would have had no time to rest after the long journey.

Cotton planting in northern Alabama started early in the year, as early as April. Dred probably heard all about it from Job Key's slaves. The Key place was the closest plantation. Where the two plantations met and where wagons and plows turned around, a small piece of land had been set aside. It was a cemetery for slaves. If Dred needed any proof that life in Alabama could be hard and unhealthy, he had only to look at the dirt mounds in that section of ground.

Dred and the other field slaves put in that first crop of cotton. Cotton needs close tending. After a month or so of growing, the plants must be thinned out. And that means hours and days of work in the hot sun. All of Peter Blow's slaves, from old Solomon down to the very youngest, were probably there with Dred, stooping and picking and weeding, the sun pounding on their shoulders

Slave children were sent to work in the fields as soon as they were big enough to carry water or drag a cotton sack.

and backs. Tall green cotton plants with yellow-pink blooms were bobbing in Peter Blow's fields that June, proof of Dred and the other slaves' hard work.

Then tragedy struck. The boom turned into a panic. Years of war and bad harvests in Europe had driven up the prices for American products. But the coming of peace and good weather brought better harvests in Europe–and less demand for American cotton. Cotton prices fell like a bucket dropped down a well. A pound of cotton had brought twenty-five cents before Peter Blow pulled up stakes in Virginia. Now he'd be lucky if he got half that much.

You couldn't start an Alabama plantation without borrowing money, not unless you were rich. And Dred's master certainly wasn't. You could spend thousands of dollars just on land in the 1830s. Then you needed slaves to work it. A good field hand went for more than five hundred dollars. Even with slaves like Dred walking all the way, it cost a good thousand dollars in food and other expenses to bring them to Alabama. Tools and seed and farm animals cost thousands more. Peter Blow hadn't been in Alabama much more than six months, and he was already looking at a pile of debt.

A year or two of hard work did nothing to erase that debt. Peter Blow needed to raise some cash, and quickly. In early 1821, he borrowed two thousand dollars from John Jones of Madison County, where Huntsville was the county seat. If he couldn't pay back the loan in cash money, he promised to pay Jones in slaves.

Peter Blow's agreement with Jones listed eight slaves. There was Solomon, the oldest at sixty. Hannah was then about forty-five. Then there were the field slaves: Luke, Will, and Sam, all in their twenties, and Dred, about sixteen. At thirteen, Isaac was old enough to carry water to the fields, run errands, and take care of other chores. Phillis was the only other slave, a young woman about Dred's age. She may have worked for the mistress at the big house. She probably helped in the fields at harvest-time, too. And she may have been the wife Dred talked of years and years later. The one, he said, whom his master sold away from him when he was a young fellow.

Peter Blow's slaves could not have felt very secure, knowing about the agreement he'd made. Blow took out another loan in the spring. Once again, Blow said that if he couldn't find the money, he'd repay the loan in slaves. He listed the same eight slaves. But Isaac and Phillis were never mentioned again in Peter Blow's records. Most likely, they were sold. The land, too, was finally sold in December for five thousand dollars. The new owner got it at a bargain price—a price that covered Peter Blow's debts and left a little to spare.

Dred's master was looking for a place to start over—again. He thought he had found it in Florence, a bustling new town near a group of shoals and islands and waterfalls on the Tennessee River. Florence seemed to have sprung up out of nothing in the three years since its founding. Town lots were selling like hot-cakes. Buildings were going up left and right. As one visitor put it that July, "It is not uncommon to see a framed building begun in the morning and finished by night."

Some slave families were not divided and sold. This 1862 photograph shows five generations of a slave family, all born on the plantation of J. J. Smith of Beaufort, South Carolina.

By the time Dred moved with his master to Florence, probably
in late 1821, he was full grown, almost eighteen years old and
around five feet tall. In Florence his master didn't buy farmland.
Instead, Blow rented a large house, right in the middle of town.
And he put out a sign for the Peter Blow Inn. Unable to succeed
as a cotton farmer, he was ready to try his luck as an innkeeper.

Lots of travelers stopped in Florence, Alabama, in the 1820s.
Some were looking for opportunities in the growing town. Others
were headed upriver to Huntsville. Still more were taking a meal or
a rest before journeying back downriver on the flatboats and other
craft that brought supplies and animals and people to Florence.

Peter Blow's inn did well enough. Even an old slave like Solomon
would be a help carrying luggage and serving at dinnertime.
Hannah could cook and do the laundry. Mrs. Blow could super-
vise the Blow girls—Elizabeth, Charlotte, and Patsey—who were
all old enough now to help out. (The oldest girl, Mary Anne, had
stayed behind in Huntsville, marrying a young man there.) With
all that help, Peter Blow may have hired out some of his slaves to
work as field hands. Other whites "rented" slaves from masters
who didn't need their labor at home or who needed cash money
more than labor. But Dred wasn't hired out, as far as we know.

At the Peter Blow Inn, Dred was the hostler, the man in charge
of caring for travelers' horses. Perhaps in back of the house there
was a barn where Dred tended to the horses. Wherever Dred did
his work, he was bound to have company. Taylor Blow, the first
in the newest crop of Blow boys, was a toddler, born just before
the family left Huntsville. William Thomas Blow was born not

long after the move. And then there were the older boys. In 1821, young Peter was seven and Henry Taylor was four. Dred probably helped raise them, just as he had the other Blow boys back in Southampton County.

Virginia must have seemed a world away to Dred and those boys. Even the oldest boy, Peter, had only hazy memories of home. But Dred could answer the boys' questions about the Olde Place and Tower Hill. He could tell them about the firecrackers set off each year at Christmas and about the dusty red dirt roads and buzzing cicadas in summer. He could tell them, too, about the boys who'd been buried back in the red soil of Southampton County.

In that way, at least, the Blows had been luckier in Alabama. Only one Blow had to be buried. Mary Anne died in Huntsville just a few short years after her family moved on to Florence.

The Blows kept moving, but not far. In 1827, Peter Blow bought first one lot, then part of another, sitting across from each other on Pine Street in Florence. The Peter Blow Inn, it seemed, would have a more permanent home, and so would the Blows and their slaves. But Peter Blow still dreamed of becoming wealthy. He had one more big move to get out of his system. And where he went, his family and his slaves went, too.

CHAPTER TWO

Big Changes

CONSIDERING HOW MUCH MONEY PETER BLOW HAD lost farming cotton in Huntsville, he might have been content to stay in Florence and be an innkeeper. After all, he was doing well there. The lots he'd bought for about six hundred dollars just three years before were worth two thousand dollars by 1830. But he could make a good profit if he sold them. And if he succeeded as an innkeeper in a small town like Florence, he might do even better in a big city. In the southwest in 1830, the biggest and most exciting city around was St. Louis, Missouri.

Founded by the French in the 1760s, St. Louis was fast becoming an altogether American town. It was a gateway to the West for pioneers. It was a major port on the country's greatest river, the Mississippi. Hundreds of steamboats—and hundreds more keelboats and other craft—stopped at the crowded levee each year. They emptied out and took on cargo. This cargo included human beings, for St. Louis carried on a busy trade in black slaves.

Some white travelers to the city and its slave market spent the night at the Jefferson Hotel. That was the name Peter Blow gave to the house he rented on Pine Street, just west of Main.

St. Louis was a much bigger city than the Blows and Dred were used to. Like Florence, it was booming. Brick buildings

BIG CHANGES

St. Louis grew rapidly in the 1830s. The city was a popular spot for explorers
to gather supplies before departing on western expeditions.

were going up all over. The air filled with the stink of the brick-
making furnaces and the choking smoke of thousands of coal- or
wood-fired stoves. The city was rarely quiet, with a constant
hustle and bustle. The city could also be a dangerous place, for
diseases spread quickly in the crowded streets, hitting slaves
especially hard.

Dred may have taken care of guests' horses, just as he had
done in Florence. He may have been sent to gather coal to heat
their rooms. And he may have shouldered their bags when they
came up from the levee to the Jefferson Hotel.

Slaves never knew from one day to the next if they would be sold at
an auction and taken far away from their family.

It would have been hard for a visitor to St. Louis to miss seeing
a slave auction. Some slaves were sold right on the courthouse
steps. Still more were auctioned off at various slave pens downtown. In the 1830s, slavery was against the law in the North, but
it was legal in many southern states, including Missouri. In St.
Louis, white visitors came to a slave market just to watch the
lively display and sale of children, mothers, and fathers. "How
much is offered for this woman?" a dealer would yell. "She is a
good cook, good washer, a good obedient servant. She has got
religion!" The slaves were cleaned and dressed to look their best

for a quick sale. Older ones had their hair blackened with polish
to hide any gray. All were told to stand still as slave buyers poked
and prodded them and checked for healthy teeth. But no matter
how the dealers tried to pretty things up, the place stank of fear.
You could see it in the slaves' faces.

Before Dred had been in St. Louis for long, he probably saw
slaves on the auction block, some heading north to work on the
frontier, most being sold south to work on plantations. In the
early 1830s, Dred may have traveled south many times—but not
to pick cotton. Peter Blow is said to have hired him out to work
on steamboats traveling the Mississippi River. Blow needed the
money more than he needed slaves at the hotel. He was feeling
poor, as usual, and now he was "slave poor," as the expression
went. He had more slaves than he could use at home and no other
property to speak of. If he wanted to raise some cash, he would
have to sell a slave.

Solomon was too old. By 1830, he was nearly seventy, and few
slaves ever dreamed of living that long. Hannah was in her mid-
fifties, also old for a slave. Luke was always a family favorite, a
slave who'd gotten "religion." (As another slave put it, "religion"
in Missouri consisted of "teaching the slave that he must never
strike a white man; that God made him a slave; and that, when
whipped, he must not find fault.")

Dred and Sam and Will seemed likeliest to be sold. They were
in their late twenties and early thirties, prime years for male
slaves. Peter Blow thought they might fetch prime dollars. And
he could certainly use the cash. Shortly after the Blows moved to

St. Louis, Mrs. Blow died. A proper funeral cost a lot of money. Soon Charlotte Blow had met a young man named Joseph Charless–which was good news–but a wedding, like a funeral, cost money.

In the summer of 1831, a young army doctor named John Emerson made a payment to Peter Blow. Emerson wanted to buy a slave to take with him when he was posted to U.S. government forts as a doctor. Emerson's payment was small, so the doctor may not have taken ownership of a slave all at once. But the money could have covered some of the bills that piled up after Mrs. Blow's funeral. It could have paid for a fine wedding dinner for Charlotte. And it most certainly spelled big changes for Dred.

We don't know how Peter Blow went about giving Dred the news. But slaves often knew when a big change was coming. If Mistress took you to a room apart from the others and offered you a place to sit down, you knew. If Master said he wanted to talk to you about something but kept avoiding your eyes, you knew.

Dred was sold to Dr. Emerson, and there wasn't a thing he could do about it. Dred knew he might never see Solomon, Hannah, Luke, Will, or Sam again. There was no way he could change that. But sometime in 1833, he ran off from Emerson and hid for a while in the Lucas Swamps, on the outskirts of St. Louis. Dred stayed a runaway long enough for Dr. Emerson to make a complaint to the Blows. Finally Dred came back. Maybe he thought that if he couldn't change things, he'd better make the best of them.

By the fall of 1833 Dred and his new master were on their way up the Mississippi River. Dr. Emerson had been working hard

When Dred moved to Fort Armstrong with Dr. Emerson, he traveled north
for the first time, leaving the familiar southern landscape and warm weather
to face the wilderness and its harsh winters.

to get a good job as an army doctor. Finally, all his letters and
requests had paid off. He was posted to Fort Armstrong at Rock
Island, Illinois, arriving there on December 1, 1833.

Slavery was illegal in the state of Illinois, but Dred went to the
fort with Dr. Emerson anyway. Officers and others at the fort were
allowed to keep "servants." The U.S. government even helped
officers cover the costs of feeding and clothing their servants at
frontier forts. No one much worried if most of those servants
were actually slaves. A paid white servant would surely run off
and stake a claim to land around the fort. A black slave might
run off, but he or she would most likely be captured by whites
who hoped to get a reward or who sold slaves in nearby southern states.

DRED AND HARRIET SCOTT

If Dred knew that he was technically "free" in Illinois, he never did anything about it. He never tried to run off. Apart from disappearing for a while into the Lucas Swamps, Dred didn't let on how angry he was or wasn't about his life. Slaves rarely did. Complaining, "uppity" slaves were likely to be sold and sent south to pick cotton. Dred had already done plenty of that.

Dred and Dr. Emerson made for an odd pair. They were about the same age, but Dred was black and small and a southerner. John Emerson was a pale, gangly six feet four with his boots off. He was a Yankee from Pennsylvania with a white-hot temper. Like Peter Blow, Dred's new master was never content where he was. Almost from the moment he set foot at Fort Armstrong, John Emerson was asking for a better posting.

At the fort, Dred's master quickly put him to work. Dr. Emerson found that the room he was supposed to use as a hospital and office was so unhealthy it made his patients sicker. He had Dred set up tents until something better could be built. The doctor was busy, but not so busy that he couldn't stake his own claim to land in nearby Bettendorf, Iowa. He likely sent Dred to work that claim and build a rough cabin there. Before long, however, Emerson's pleas for a better post brought results. In the spring of 1836, Fort Armstrong was shut down. Army surgeon John Emerson, along with his slave Dred, would soon report to Fort Snelling, in Indian country.

CHAPTER THREE

Meeting Harriet

IN 1836, DRED WAS ABOUT THIRTY-THREE YEARS OLD. He had lived in four states. His first master had taken him from the warm, humid Virginia of their birth to the even more tropical Alabama cotton belt. Missouri had a more temperate climate, but St. Louis still simmered and sweated in the summer. Dred's quarters at Fort Armstrong were as drafty and damp as any he had ever lived in, but the cold of northwestern Illinois made them seem worse. Now he was headed to a place already well known for its bitter winters. The trip to Fort Snelling, located in what is now Minnesota, would take Dred away from everything he had ever known.

The change was obvious as the steamer *Missouri Fulton* carried Dr. Emerson, Dred, and others north on the Mississippi River in early May. Galena, in the northwest corner of Illinois, was a tiny town, but it was a huge city compared to other settlements along the river there. Farther north, the travelers entered Wisconsin Territory. (This vast tract of land would later be carved up to form the states of Wisconsin, Minnesota, Iowa, North Dakota, and South Dakota.)

Finally, when Dred and the others on the deck of the *Missouri Fulton* thought they might never see another cabin—let alone

Many travelers rode steamboats up and down the Mississippi River, which provided the easiest route north and south in the mid-1800s.

another town–the boat rounded a bend. There, on a high bluff overlooking the meeting of the Mississippi and the St. Peter's Rivers, stood a glimmering-white, limestone-walled fort. And above Fort Snelling's grassy parade ground the stars and stripes flew, marking a tiny American outpost on Indian land.

Slavery wasn't legal in Wisconsin Territory, where Fort Snelling was located. But as at Fort Armstrong, no one gave the officers there any trouble about having slaves. Slaves were just another piece of property. Plus, the territory around the fort was all prairies and rivers and Indians. It wasn't a place where you could hire servants easily. Slaves seemed the best solution to that problem.

Officers on their way to Fort Snelling often bought slaves in St. Louis before traveling the last seven hundred or so miles north. One boy whose family was posted to the fort in the 1830s remembered buying slaves after stocking up on ham, dried beef, rice, furniture, and wine. "At St. Louis," he recalled, "the last of our necessary purchases was made, to wit: a nice-looking yellow [light-skinned] girl and an uncommonly black man."

Even if Dred knew that slavery was illegal in U.S. territories, a runaway slave had little chance of surviving. Fort Snelling was a cold place, even in May. In mid-June, after Dred's arrival, one resident wrote in his journal, "Weather very unpleasant . . . *fires* found agreeable, in fact *indispensible.*"

Fort Snelling was located on the edge of wilderness. Wolves prowled outside the stone walls that winter, treading a path in the snow. Less than a year before Dred arrived, ten bears had been shot just a few miles away from the fort, at Lake Calhoun.

Fort Snelling was a lonesome place. The garrison had been built to house many men, but much of it stood empty in 1836. Dred was one of perhaps fifteen or twenty blacks living there. Black or white, the number of people living at the fort was small compared to the number of Indians who lived outside.

Every day, a steady stream of mainly Dakota Indians came to talk with Major Lawrence Taliaferro [tol-UH-ver], the Indian agent. The U.S. government paid Taliaferro to keep the peace with the Indians who lived beyond the fort's stone walls. Some Dakota came to the agency wearing simple blankets, others "splendidly equipt with beautiful head dress & other ornaments of dress."

Surrounded by wilderness, Fort Snelling was built between 1820 and 1825. It soon became a popular spot where Indians and fur traders gathered for supplies.

Some of the soldiers learned their language, but their words would have been strange to Dred.

Inside the walls of the fort, things weren't quite so strange and lonesome. Dred soon knew everyone there. It was hard *not* to know everything about your neighbors in such an isolated place. As a woman who spent her childhood at the fort later recalled, "[F]ew know how closely drawn together are the occupants of a frontier post, how, like one family, they hear each other's griefs and share each other's joys." Dred's great joy in coming to Fort Snelling that May was meeting Harriet. She was so serious-looking and sure of herself that Dred must have thought she was older. But there she was, only about seventeen years old; Dred was nearly twice her age.

Harriet had arrived at the fort a few years earlier. She was the slave of Major Taliaferro, brought to the fort from her master's family home in Virginia. Taliaferro's stone house was located nearby, on a small rise outside the fort's walls. Harriet probably lived there with Taliaferro and his other slaves.

Indian agent Major Lawrence Taliaferro brought his slave
Harriet Robinson to Fort Snelling in about 1835.

As a slave, Harriet went by one name only, just plain Harriet. But years later, her former master Major Taliaferro called her Harriet Robinson, and that was the name she gave herself. Perhaps Robinson was the name of the family that had owned Harriet's mother. Perhaps it was the family name of her original white owners. It's possible: a Robinson family lived close to the Taliaferros in Virginia. Harriet's name is as mysterious as the rest of her life before she met Dred.

The two slaves married soon after they met. Marriage among slaves was commonplace. Laws in many southern states made it illegal for slaves to have an official wedding, with a justice of the peace, but slaves married anyway. They called their ceremony "jumping the broom," since the couple said their vows and then hopped over a broom handle as a pair, entering their new life together. But Dred and Harriet either didn't jump the broom, or they did and had a "white" wedding, too. Harriet's master, Major Taliaferro, was also a justice of the peace. And sometime between May 1836, when the two first met, and fall 1837, Major Taliaferro officiated at Dred and Harriet's wedding.

The slaves of two different masters couldn't marry and live together without some property being sold. So the major sold Harriet to John Emerson, and from then on the two were known as "Dr. Emerson's slaves." It's not certain where they lived, but a likely spot is a cellar room under the fort's hospital and Dr. Emerson's quarters. Much of the fort was built on a bank, with cellars underneath. The hospital cellars had wood floors, small glass-paned windows, and walk-out doors. Too bad the cellars

Dred lived in free territory for almost nine years, including the time he
spent at Fort Snelling as Dr. Emerson's slave.

didn't face south to catch some sun-warmth. The rooms had
brick fireplaces, but as Dred and Harriet must have discovered,
an open fire was no match for the cold of a Minnesota winter or
blasts of the north wind.

Together, the couple survived that first winter and settled into
the rhythm of fort life. Each morning, the flag went up the pole
to the roll of a drum. Each night, the sentinel called out "All's
well around." And in between, enlisted men lined up for roll call
and then went off to do their work of the day. For most, that
meant work not too different from what Dred had done as a
slave. The men chopped wood for winter fires, often carrying it
great distances across the high-grass prairie to the fort. They
tended corn, potatoes, turnips, and onions in the fort's large gardens. They harvested hay from nearby marshes to feed livestock.

Only occasionally did they have to do military work, helping keep peace between the Indians.

In some ways, Dred and Harriet had more freedom at Fort Snelling than enlisted men did. They never had to show up for roll call. They most likely worked in the fort's gardens, took care of animals around the fort, and did the cooking, cleaning, and washing. But they probably didn't have to do the more backbreaking work of gathering cordwood and haying in wet marshland. And if they didn't follow orders, they weren't lashed with a cat-'o-nine-tails, prodded with bayonets, and then sent out into the wilderness to live or die, as disobedient soldiers were.

But in another way, perhaps the most important way, Dred and Harriet were not free. Dr. Emerson, Major Taliaferro, and all the other whites they knew looked upon them as property, like a good horse or a well-made piece of furniture. If a white officer had a disobedient slave, that slave would be sold. Most likely that slave would be sent south to St. Louis on the next steamboat with instructions to be auctioned off at one of the markets downtown.

Dred and Harriet had to live with that fear. But they also may have had some small reason for hope. That hope lay in what happened to a slave called Rachael. Rachael had lived at Fort Snelling in the early 1830s, in the house next door to Taliaferro's. She had been brought to the post by the Indian subagent, Elias Langham. Not long after, her new owner, an army lieutenant, took her to St. Louis. Once there, Rachael filed suit in court. She claimed that because her master had taken her to live in places, such as Fort Snelling, where slavery was illegal, she was no longer a slave. In June 1836, Rachael won her freedom and that of her child, Jarvis, who'd been delivered by Dr. Jarvis, Dr. Emerson's predecessor at the fort.

Dred and Harriet surely knew of Rachael's story, but they did not immediately follow her example and seek their freedom. That September, Dr. Emerson hired Harriet out to Lieutenant James Thompson and his wife, Catherine. Harriet worked for the couple for a few months, and Thompson paid Emerson for his slave's work. Then Harriet was hired out again, to the post commander, Major Joseph Plympton. Dred may have been hired out, too. If he was, no one kept a record of it. It was hard always trying to please new masters and mistresses. But soon both Dred and Harriet were facing bigger changes. In November 1837, Dr. Emerson was transferred to Fort Jesup in Louisiana.

He didn't take Harriet and Dred with him at first. In his haste to get to his newest appointment, Emerson canoed partway down the Mississippi. His slaves stayed behind, hired out to others at the fort. Who knew when he'd call for them? But Harriet and Dred knew that they would likely be heading south soon.

Fort Jesup was near the Sabine River, the natural border between Louisiana and Texas. It was bayou country, wet and hot and boggy. It was also slave country, and part of the purpose of having a fort there was to help put down slave rebellions. It was something of a wilderness, but there were towns and cities not too far off. Dr. Emerson settled into his quarters at the hospital and soon found friends among the officers. One officer, Lieutenant Henry Bainbridge, was married to a pleasant woman from a good St. Louis family. Her younger sister, Eliza Irene Sanford, was visiting the fort that winter. Dr. Emerson knew a good match when he saw one, and he made short work of courting Irene. The two were married on February 6, 1838. Not long after, Emerson sent for his slaves.

By April, Dred and Harriet were in Louisiana, most likely having traveled the hundreds of miles south without their master. It couldn't have been the easiest trip, especially for Harriet. She was in the early stages of pregnancy, a time when miscarriages frequently happen. But the baby and Harriet managed well enough. The long Louisiana summer was also a struggle for the slave couple. Harriet grew more and more pregnant as the days grew hotter and hotter. But when her time drew near, another threat to her baby's health arose. Her master, Dr. Emerson, had been transferred once again—this time back north to Fort Snelling.

In the 1830s, doctors only rarely assisted at births. Bringing babies into the world was considered women's work, not something worthy of a doctor's years of training. But Dr. Emerson may have been forced to pitch in when Harriet and Dred had their first child. Eliza was born on the small steamboat *Gypsy* that carried Emerson, his wife, and his slaves up the Mississippi River in October 1838. The boat was just north of the state of Missouri when the little girl was born. But though she was born in free country, Eliza, as the child of slaves, was also considered a slave. She belonged to Dr. Emerson the same way his trunks of books and cases of medical tools did.

Dred and Harriet endured cold winters in their quarters, which were
probably located beneath the hospital at Fort Snelling.

Dred and Harriet were luckier than some slave parents. Their
master seemed to care about his new property. When a supply of
small cast-iron stoves arrived at Fort Snelling, John Emerson
asked for one—for his slaves. Perhaps he was concerned about
the baby's chances of surviving in the cold. Perhaps he figured
that any heat in his cellar was bound to rise up and keep him
toasty, too. Whatever his reasons, Dr. Emerson stubbornly insisted that his slaves should have a stove, just as the officers of
the fort did. (Enlisted men slept twelve to a room, with a poor
fire in winter.)

When the quartermaster turned down Emerson's request, saying
there weren't enough stoves left, the doctor called him a liar. A

full-blown fight followed, with the quartermaster hitting Emerson right between the eyes and Emerson racing off to find his pistol. The commanding officer, Major Plympton, finally stopped Dred and Harriet's master from making himself look even more foolish. Plympton disarmed the doctor and put him on house arrest to cool his temper.

Whether Dred and Harriet and Eliza got their stove, we'll never know. But they did live through the winter of 1838 and '39, and the following winter, too. By May 1840, however, they were on the move again. For months, Dr. Emerson had been begging his superiors for a better posting. Finally, they answered by sending him to the wilds of Florida, where the United States was fighting a war against the Seminole Indians. It was a *different* posting, but surely no better than Fort Snelling.

Mrs. Emerson didn't relish the idea of going along with her husband, not to an untamed wilderness where a war was raging. It wouldn't be safe for her, or for Dr. Emerson's valuable property— his slaves. Irene Emerson returned to her family home, a plantation a dozen miles outside of St. Louis. Dred and Harriet and Eliza stayed in the city, where they were hired out for wages.

St. Louis was full of slaves who hired out. Some were expected to find their own positions, as laundresses and cooks, as helpers on steamboats, and as workers on the huge city levee. Dred and Harriet may have found their own jobs, but they didn't take home the wages. Instead, Mrs. Emerson or her father collected the yearly fee. It was up to the people who hired slaves to see to their lodgings and food. Usually, hired slaves lived in a back

room of a white person's shop or home, or in one of the shacks
or lean-tos that sprouted up in St. Louis's alleys.

As slaves, Dred and Harriet had known uncertainty before,
but in the early 1840s, their lives—and the status of their young
family—became even more precarious. Sometime in the 1840s,
Dred and Harriet lost two baby boys. Harriet had always worked
during pregnancy—all slaves did—even though resting might
have kept her babies healthy and stopped them from being born
too early to survive. Eliza was healthy, but St. Louis was full of
sickness, especially in the hot summer months.

In the middle of a hot, hot August in 1842, Dr. Emerson left
Florida. He'd been asking for months for a better position. Per-
haps he'd asked one time too often. For Dr. Emerson hadn't left
Florida of his own free will. He'd been discharged from the army.

When he turned up in St. Louis late that summer, he spent
hours firing off letters to anyone in the army who had ever
helped him before. He wanted his old job back, even in swampy,
sweaty Florida. But the army didn't want Dr. Emerson back.

Emerson didn't have an easy time setting up a private practice
as a doctor. Everyone around St. Louis seemed to have heard that
he'd been fired from his job as an army surgeon. But he still had
some land in Davenport, Iowa, near old Fort Armstrong. It was
possible the news of his discharge hadn't reached Iowa yet, so
Emerson took his wife there in 1843. He didn't take his slaves
along. An army surgeon could get away with having slave "servants" at an army post in one of the territories. But Dr. Emerson
was a civilian now, and slavery was illegal in Iowa.

Dred and Harriet and Eliza most likely stayed on in St. Louis, still hired out for pay. Perhaps Dred thought that once Dr. Emerson left the army he would free his slaves. Certainly some of the officers Dred and Harriet had known at Fort Snelling had freed their "servants" after they had left the army. For them, slaves were a temporary solution to the problem of getting good help on the frontier. When they moved back to one of the states, where free blacks and whites worked for pay as servants, they no longer needed or wanted slaves. Dr. Emerson may not have wanted his slaves, but he surely needed them.

As an army surgeon, he had made good money, good enough to support a wife who was used to nice things. But as a doctor trying to set up a practice in Davenport, he was struggling. He and Irene had another mouth to feed when their daughter, Henrietta, was born in 1843. Emerson needed all the income he could get, and that included the money he received hiring out Dred and Harriet for wages. In a year or so, he could count on earning a little for Eliza's work, too, if she was strong. In fact, Emerson stood to make even more money by selling the little girl. A slave's value was all in her potential to grow up and work hard. Slave dealers would look on Eliza as "young and likely." Her parents might sell for five hundred dollars apiece, although at forty, Dred was already past his prime. But Eliza herself might fetch up to three hundred and fifty dollars.

Did Dr. Emerson intend to free his slaves or sell them? We'll never know. He died just after Christmas in 1843. His widow, Irene, came from a family that, as a rule, didn't free slaves. The

Sanfords only sold a slave when he or she was too troublesome to keep. Knowing that an uppity slave was likely to be sold down the river to work and die on a cotton plantation kept the others in line.

When Irene Sanford Emerson inherited Dred and Harriet and Eliza, she didn't change much about their lives. She kept on hiring out her late husband's slaves, but she made sure she kept things in the family. Her sister Mary's husband, Captain Henry Bainbridge, was by then serving at Jefferson Barracks, just outside St. Louis. Dred and Harriet and Eliza were hired out to work for Bainbridge. In about a year, the captain was posted to Texas, where yet another war was brewing. Eliza and Harriet may have stayed in St. Louis, but Dred probably went with Bainbridge to Corpus Christi and then to Matamoros in 1845 and 1846.

By early 1846, Dred was back with his family at Jefferson Barracks, still acting as Bainbridge's servant. Harriet was expecting another baby, and it was good to have all the family together when the little girl was born that March. Lizzie, as she was called, was lucky. She was as healthy as her seven-year-old big sister, Eliza. But she was unlucky, too. Lizzie was born in the slave state of Missouri. Could she and the rest of her family ever hope to be free?

NEW HAMPSHIRE
VERMONT
MAINE

WISCONSIN
TERRITORY

Fort Snelling

Mississippi

MASSACHUSETTS

IOWA TERRITORY

MICHIGAN

NEW YORK

RHODE ISLAND
CONNECTICUT

PENNSYLVANIA

NEW JERSEY

Bettendorf

DELAWARE

Rock Island

OHIO

INDIANA

ILLINOIS

King George County

MARYLAND

River

VIRGINIA

MISSOURI

St. Louis

Southampton County

UNORGANIZED
TERRITORY

KENTUCKY

NORTH CAROLINA

TENNESSEE

ARKANSAS

SOUTH
CAROLINA

Florence

Huntsville

MISSISSIPPI

ALABAMA

GEORGIA

REPUBLIC
OF TEXAS

Fort Jesup

LOUISIANA

FLORIDA
TERRITORY

Corpus Christi

◆ Dred's travels

Matamoros

✧ Harriet's travels

❖ Dred and Harriet's travels

Slave state or territory

Free state

Free territory

Dred and Harriet Scott's travels in both free and slave states and
territories, 1800–1850.

CHAPTER FOUR

Young and Likely

SOMETIME IN THE MID-1840s, DRED AND HARRIET started looking hard at their family's future. They had lost two babies already. Those little boys died from the harshness of slavery. Dred and Harriet couldn't bear to think of losing their girls, too. Eliza was close to the age of the children who stood on auction blocks in St. Louis—the ones the slave traders called "young and likely." The ones who brought top dollar.

Dr. Emerson had cared enough about his slave property to fight to keep Dred and Harriet and Eliza warm when they lived at Fort Snelling. He had been a good enough master to them that they had never tried to run away, even when they had been hired out in St. Louis and might have escaped to Illinois, a free state just across the river. Mrs. Emerson may have been a kind mistress or a terrible one. We'll never know for certain. But we do know that about the time Lizzie was born, Dred asked his mistress for his freedom.

He was willing to pay for it. As other slaves had done before, he was proposing to buy a piece of property—himself. He would pay over a period of time, perhaps several years. He also meant to buy freedom for his wife and daughters. Dred offered Mrs. Emerson some money up front. Then, he gave the name of "an

Dred lived at Jefferson Barracks while working for
Captain Henry Bainbridge.

eminent citizen of St. Louis, an officer in the army, as security for
the payment of the remainder."

That army officer was probably Captain Henry Bainbridge,
Mrs. Emerson's own brother-in-law. Bainbridge had been Dred
and Harriet's master-for-hire for at least three years. He'd joined a
southern slave-holding family when he married Irene Emerson's
sister Mary in 1821. But Bainbridge was a Yankee. Buying and
selling slaves was illegal in his home state of New Jersey. Dred
spoke well of Bainbridge in later years, calling him a "good
man." Perhaps Bainbridge was good enough to help Dred and
Harriet in their quest for freedom.

If he was, it's likely his sister-in-law Irene didn't appreciate his "help." She had no intention of letting her slaves buy their freedom. As one man said later, "people of good standing"–people like Irene Emerson–"did not market [sell] their negroes except as punishment." Slaves were a good source of income. Although Mrs. Emerson was living comfortably at her father's plantation, she had a young child to think of. Dred and Harriet and Eliza– and now Lizzie–were part of Henrietta Emerson's inheritance.

In just a few days' time, Irene Emerson hired out Dred and Harriet to Samuel and Adeline Russell, part owners of a grocery business called Russell and Bennett. It was located at 82 Water Street in St. Louis. Harriet must have had a hard time of it, changing masters just as she was getting used to mothering a newborn again. Eliza probably helped out when Harriet couldn't do her share of the work at the wholesale grocery. Dred most likely made deliveries around the city, picked up new stock at the levee, and did heavy lifting and carrying for Samuel Russell and his partner. Irene Emerson must have been relieved to have her slaves safely away from her Yankee brother-in-law's meddling, but her troubles with Dred and Harriet were only beginning.

ON APRIL 6, 1846, two petitions were filed in Missouri Circuit Court in St. Louis. In one, a man named Dred Scott stated that he was "entitled to his freedom." He based his claim on the fact that he had been taken by his former master, Dr. John Emerson, into territories where slavery was illegal. When Dr. Emerson brought

Dred to Fort Armstrong and Fort Snelling–both places where slavery was illegal–Dred should have become free.

The second petition, filed by "Harriet, a woman of color," used much the same argument. She had, she claimed, been brought from Virginia to Fort Snelling by Major Taliaferro. There, she had been sold to Dr. Emerson. And, because her masters had held her in a territory of the United States, where slavery was illegal, she, too, was free.

Any good lawyer looking at the facts of Dred and Harriet's life together would have told them they had a promising case. Ten years before, Rachael, the slave from Fort Snelling, had successfully gained her freedom in a St. Louis court. Most previous cases of slaves taken into territories or states where slavery was illegal had ended with the same verdict: freedom for the slaves.

But why file petitions in the spring of 1846? And why make a point, as Dred did in his petition, of listing the last name *Scott?* Dred and Harriet may have been using the last name Scott for some time, but this was the first official document bearing the name. It's likely that when Harriet filed her petition, she gave the last name Scott, too. But a white clerk in the slaveholding south was unlikely to treat a black slave woman with respect. A last name suggested that someone like Harriet might be a person, not a piece of property. Still, Harriet must have tried to get white people to call her by her full name. In later court documents, one clerk marked out her last name when he saw his mistake.

John Emerson's former slaves were trying very hard to be treated as people, not property. It was clear from what they called themselves. It was clear from the petitions they filed that April. But the two best reasons for filing suit that spring were Eliza and Lizzie. Those girls were the best reasons in the world to file for freedom.

The status of children under slavery followed that of their mother. If Harriet were judged to be a slave, her children were slaves, too. But if she won her suit, then her girls were as free as she was. And they had a whole lifetime to enjoy that freedom. They'd never have to be someone's "servant" when they were really no more to their master or mistress than a well-made piece of furniture or a good horse. They would never have to move when their master or mistress decided. They might go where they wished, when they wished. And most importantly, they need never fear being sold on the auction block.

Surely the Scotts knew of the house on Morgan and Garrison Streets. The woman who lived there did a tidy business buying up slave babies as young as Lizzie. She bought them just when they had been weaned from the breast, or just before their mothers were auctioned off. She raised them until they were big enough to do small jobs, then sold them at a city slave market.

Prices for slaves had been climbing steadily. By the mid-1800s, a female slave like Harriet, in good health and not too old, would bring a thousand dollars on the slave market. Even Dred, in his forties, would bring a good price. Still, if Mrs. Emerson had wanted to sell her two older slaves, she might have hesitated. People who bought slaves wanted to be sure that the slaves didn't have any problems related to past ownership. Just as people buying a house nowadays check the title, or ownership, before making a down payment, people in the 1800s checked the titles of slaves like Harriet and Dred. Those years spent in the territories would spell trouble to any new owner.

The titles for the two girls—Eliza and Lizzie Scott—were less troublesome. Both girls were too young to know how to file petitions in court. If they were sold quickly and far away, they or their parents had little chance of arguing their case before a judge. Moreover, Lizzie was born in a slave state. As for Eliza's place of birth, that was just her word against that of her white owner.

If Mrs. Emerson was looking for a source of money or if she was simply looking to unload some property, selling the Scott daughters was a place to start. And in about 1846, Irene Emerson was talking about moving away from St. Louis. She was still young and hoped to remarry. The best way for her to meet eligible men was to visit one of her married sisters and meet her brother-in-law's unmarried friends. Irene Emerson chose not to visit with her sister Mary (and Mary's meddling husband, Captain Bainbridge) this time. Instead, she was planning to travel to Springfield, Massachusetts, to stay with another sister, Mrs. James Barnes. Massachusetts was not a place for slaves. Slavery had been illegal there since 1783, and the state was home to a number of people who opposed slavery, called abolitionists.

The Scotts may or may not have known about Mrs. Emerson's plans. But they didn't want to risk losing Eliza and Lizzie. Free blacks or the minister at Harriet's church may have encouraged

Dred sought freedom for himself and his family, first offering to buy freedom from their master, Irene Emerson, then asking the courts to set them free.

the Scotts to seek their freedom just as Rachael had done–in the courts.

Harriet Scott was a member of the Second African Baptist Church of St. Louis. The Reverend John R. Anderson ministered to the small group of blacks who met at Third and Cherry Streets. Reverend Anderson was a free man, but many members of his church were slaves. Sometimes, he loaned them money to buy their freedom. Other times, he gave them encouragement.

Someone, possibly Reverend Anderson, must have introduced Harriet to a lawyer. That lawyer, Francis B. Murdoch, had filed petitions for freedom on behalf of slave women before. More women than men filed freedom suits in St. Louis. Murdoch had worked on all the usual cases: slaves promised freedom in a master's will but kept in bondage; young children snatched away from free mothers; and slaves, like Harriet, taken by their masters to places where slavery was illegal. Most with cases as strong as Harriet's had won their freedom.

After Irene Emerson refused Dred's request to buy his family, Harriet may have met with Murdoch and convinced Dred to file petitions in court. Always a take-charge person, Harriet wasn't intimidated when she had to state the facts of her life in her petition. She was surer of dates and places than Dred, and surer of herself.

But while Harriet may have started the process of petitioning for freedom in the courts, Dred found the money to pay for it. Whatever cash the family had on hand–the money Dred had promised Mrs. Emerson–it wasn't going to be enough to pay the court costs. Freedom suits took time. And in the world of lawyers and courts, time meant money. Initially, Francis Murdoch promised to cover some costs, undoubtedly with the understanding that Dred would pay him back. But Dred couldn't count on Murdoch to wait for payments. He needed to find better backers–people with money. Irene Emerson's meddling brother-in-law, Captain Bainbridge, either wasn't able or wasn't willing to lend Dred that kind of money. So Dred turned to the only other white men he'd ever shown affection for: "them boys he was raised with."

Now all grown up, the Blow boys had found some of the success and prosperity their father had chased clear across the country. Their older sister, Charlotte Blow Charless–the one whose wedding may have been paid for by Dred's sale years before–had gotten the younger boys jobs at her husband's drug and paint company. Peter Blow had found a good job on his own and married into the prominent La Beaume family of St. Louis. All in all, the Blow boys had done well for themselves. So had the Blow girls: Charlotte was wealthy and well respected in St. Louis society. Patsey had married a lawyer named Charles Drake.

By June 1847, when Dred and Harriet's cases finally made their way before a judge, Charles Drake was one of the lawyers who took statements from witnesses for Dred and Harriet before the trial. Henry Taylor Blow was one of the witnesses called to testify on Dred's behalf. One way or another, the Blows were helping out Dred and his family. Maybe the Blows felt some loyalty to their former slave. Maybe the Blows thought their former slave would need just a little help, just a little cash in order to win his freedom. When they renewed their ties with Dred Scott sometime in the mid-1840s, they couldn't have known that the Blow and the Scott families would be linked for years to come, even after Dred's death.

CHAPTER FIVE

Freedom Lost and Found and Lost Again

DRED AND HARRIET SCOTT PROBABLY DIDN'T KNOW how courts work. Their lawyers, however, knew that in Missouri slaves weren't considered to be people. Only people—usually only whites—could expect to find justice in the courts there. But when Judge John M. Krum read Dred and Harriet's petitions in April 1846, he was willing to give the Scotts the chance to argue their case in court. They just might be people, not property, after all. But they would have to prove it by making clear that their masters had taken them to territories where slavery was illegal.

It shouldn't have been difficult to prove. By June 1847, when the cases came to trial, several people had made statements, called depositions. One was Catherine Anderson, the former wife of Lieutenant Thompson at Fort Snelling. Catherine Anderson remembered hiring Harriet from Dr. Emerson in 1837. She remembered that Harriet and Dred were "universally known there to be Dr. Emerson's Slaves." Another witness, Miles Clark, recalled knowing Dred when he was at Fort Armstrong, in the free state of Illinois. Back then, according to Clark, Dred Scott "was claimed by Doctor Emerson as a slave and used by him as such."

51

The last piece of evidence came from Samuel Russell, who was still hiring the Scotts to work at his wholesale grocery business. "I hired Dred & his wife in March '46–from Mrs. Emerson," he said in a signed statement just before the trial. "I paid the hire of the servents [sic] to Mrs. Emerson. . . . " When Mrs. Emerson was out of town, Russell stated that he had paid the hire to her father, Mr. Sanford.

Dred and Harriet's freedom suit was heard in the St. Louis courthouse in 1847.

It all seemed clear. Dred and Harriet had belonged to Dr. Emerson. Now they belonged to his widow, Irene Sanford Emerson. Dr. Emerson had held them as slaves in a territory where slavery was illegal, so they should have been declared free. That was how Missouri law had worked in similar trials before. But in the courtroom that June, things didn't turn out as expected.

When Samuel Russell went on the witness stand, Irene Emerson's lawyer asked if he had personally hired Dred and Harriet. Well, no, Russell admitted, "I did not hire out the negroes myself, it was my wife who made the arrangement with Mrs. Emerson about them." Russell said further that he knew "nothing of the hiring but what I have been told by my wife." The money he'd given to Mr. Sanford he *supposed* was for the hiring of Irene Emerson's slaves. But he didn't have direct knowledge of her owning Dred and Harriet. All his knowledge, it appeared now, was secondhand.

The judge made it clear in his instructions to the jury that secondhand knowledge was worthless in court. In all that testimony, Dred and Harriet hadn't managed to prove that they were Irene Emerson's slaves. No one had come out and said directly that Dred and Harriet were being used as slaves by Mrs. Emerson.

It was a small detail. But it was a detail of enormous importance. It was significant enough to convince the jury that the Scotts weren't free. Dred and Harriet lost cases that should have been easy to win. They were still slaves, even though they hadn't proven it in court. But their lawyers told them they still had a chance at freedom. With help from the Blows, Dred and Harriet Scott had their lawyers immediately file for a new trial–a trial in which they would prove once and for all that Irene Emerson had held them as slaves. This trial, they hoped, would bring them and their daughters the freedom they craved.

One of the first things the Scotts learned about the court system was that it was slow–slower than molasses pouring on a cold day. Dred and Harriet got right to work preparing for their new trial. That July, Dred stated under oath that Samuel Russell's testimony had taken him by surprise. He went on to say that "he was & is a free man" and that a new trial would "prove that he was & is unjustly and unlawfully held in Slavery. . . ." After Dred made his statement, he and his family waited. And waited. In March 1848, the court finally granted Dred's request for a new trial.

Irene Emerson wasn't going to make any of this easy for her slaves. She put Dred and Harriet in the custody of the sheriff. He was told to hire them out for wages. Until they were hired out, they could sit in the St. Louis jail. Perhaps Reverend Anderson visited them there and tried to comfort them. (Being a minister to slaves didn't pay much, so Anderson had a paying job cleaning the jail and serving food to prisoners.)

It was expected that Harriet would earn four dollars a month and Dred would earn five. The money would be kept by the sheriff until the case was resolved one way or another. Mrs. Emerson didn't mention Eliza and Lizzie. Years later, Harriet

FREEDOM LOST AND FOUND

St. Louis's old city jail was so small that cells were often overcrowded, allowing illnesses to spread quickly among the prisoners. Dred and Harriet stayed at the jail for a time after their first trial.

told a reporter that she had sent the girls away to safety, never saying where, while the freedom suit went through the courts.

Once again, the Blow family stepped in. C. Edmund La Beaume, young Peter Blow's brother-in-law and a lawyer, hired Dred and Harriet Scott to work for him. Joseph Charless, Charlotte Blow's husband, promised to pay all court costs in the new trial. While the Scotts worked for Edmund La Beaume, they waited for their new trial to begin.

They were still waiting in 1849. Witnesses were called but couldn't be found. In May, fire destroyed part of the city of St. Louis near the waterfront. When the weather grew warmer, a deadly disease called cholera spread through the city, killing one of every ten residents. Anyone who could leave the city did so, including Irene Emerson, who finally moved to Massachusetts at about this time. But Dred and Harriet Scott couldn't leave. They had to stay on in the unhealthy city and hope for the best.

Finally, after two and a half years of waiting, in January 1850 their new trial began. This trial was the same as the first, except for one thing: Adeline Russell was a witness. But she, like her husband, was not the most convincing witness when it came to proving that Dred and Harriet Scott were slaves held by Irene Emerson. As she put it, "The only way I know these negroes belonged to Mrs. Emerson is that she hired them to me. . . ." If a better witness were to be had, Dred and Harriet's lawyers hadn't managed to find one. Her evidence, however, was good enough. On January 12, 1850, the jury declared that Dred and Harriet Scott had been slaves and that they were now free human beings.

Few people in that courtroom apart from the judges and lawyers understood all the details of law that gave Dred and Harriet their freedom. Surely many onlookers must have been mystified at how such similar trials could end with such different decisions. Irene Emerson's lawyers immediately filed for a new trial.

The interior of St. Louis's Old Courthouse has been remodeled, but Dred and Harriet's trial took place in a courtroom similar to this one.

With decisions swinging back and forth as they were, Mrs. Emerson stood a good chance of winning her slaves back. She had the money to keep fighting in court. She had the resources to make Dred and Harriet Scott's newfound freedom feel like a temporary thing. She wasn't going to let them enjoy one minute of it.

Once again, the courts moved slowly. For two years, Dred and Harriet and their daughters were—according to the courts—free people. But as long as Mrs. Emerson's appeal lasted, they were still living as slaves, hired out for wages by the sheriff. To simplify matters and cut down on time and costs, Dred and Harriet's cases had been combined into one. It was agreed that the decision in Dred's case would also cover his wife.

When the case came before the courts in 1852, the lawyers presented their arguments. Irene Emerson's lawyer, Lyman Norris, made it clear that the current trial was simply a question of property and who owned it. He asked jurors to put the question this way: what if Congress passed laws that said that owning a black horse (perfectly legal in Missouri) was illegal in the territories? If you took your black horse into the territories and brought him back to St. Louis, was he free? Just imagine that your black horse could talk: "When he comes back here and asks you to give him up [free him], would you do it?"

Dred and Harriet's lawyer took a different approach, drumming into the jurors' minds what the law said: "the taking and holding of the plaintiff [Dred Scott] as a slave at Rock Island and Fort Snelling entitled him to his freedom."

FREEDOM LOST AND FOUND

In March 1852, the Missouri Supreme Court issued its verdict: Dred Scott and his family were slaves. They'd always been slaves, and they always would be.

The court majority saw the case as a question of property. Justice William Scott wrote, "On almost three sides the State of Missouri is surrounded by free soil. . . . If a master sends his slave to hunt his horses or cattle beyond the boundary, shall he thereby be liberated?" Any law that said *yes* could cause all kinds of property disputes.

Justice Scott felt that the time had come to settle the question once and for all in favor of slave holders. "Times now are not as they were when the former decisions on this subject were made," he concluded. "Since then not only individuals but States have been possessed with a dark and fell spirit in relation to slavery." According to Justice Scott, those who wanted to end slavery (those "possessed with a dark and fell spirit" toward it) were dangerous people. Their inevitable goal, he told the courtroom, was "the overthrow and destruction of our government."

Dred and Harriet Scott were simply trying to gain their family's freedom. But all of a sudden their case had become part of a larger argument over slavery. That argument had been going on in the United States since the Constitution was drafted in 1787–since before there had been a United States of America. By the mid-1850s, the debate over whether buying and selling people was just and legal had reached a boiling point.

The debate went on, and Dred and Harriet and their children were still slaves. In less than a month, Irene Emerson's lawyers were demanding their wages from the sheriff. The Blow family must have wondered why they had gotten involved in the first place. They had spent quite a bit of money, and Dred was still a slave. Now, the supreme court was making Dred's suit seem like a case about slavery, not about one family's desire to be free.

Missouri Supreme Court Justice Hamilton Gamble disagreed with Justice William Scott, who defined slaves as property, owned by their masters whether they were in slave or free territory. Gamble said that Dr. Emerson knew slavery was illegal in the territories and it was not the fault of the court if now Dred and Harriet were freed.

But perhaps the fight was not yet over. For some time, Dred
had been hired out to work as a janitor for several law offices.
One of the offices he cleaned was upstairs on Chestnut Street, on
the sunny side of the street. It belonged to a northerner named
Roswell Field. Field didn't care much for slavery, but his beliefs
weren't so strong that he didn't do business with slave holders.
He was one of the city's most successful real estate lawyers. Every
so often, however, he took on a freedom suit. Once he got to talking with fellow lawyer Edmund La Beaume about his janitor,
Dred Scott, he became interested in the Scott family's case.

One fact in Dred's case stood out in Roswell's lawyerly mind.
Dred believed that his ownership had been transferred from
Mrs. Emerson to her brother, John Sanford, who was living in
New York. Mrs. Emerson lived in Massachusetts, and in 1850
she had remarried there. Since her departure from St. Louis,
Mrs. Emerson's brother had watched over her affairs on visits to
Missouri. Mrs. Emerson may not have signed over ownership of
the Scotts to her brother, but as far as Dred knew, John Sanford
now owned him and his family.

Roswell Field knew that the U.S. Constitution could be used
to protect the Scott family's freedom. Article 3, section 2, states
that the U.S. Supreme Court must decide controversies between
citizens of different states. When Field heard that Dred Scott of
Missouri was owned by John Sanford of New York, he realized
that a new case could be argued in front of the U.S. Supreme
Court. Dred and Harriet and Lizzie and Eliza had one more
chance at freedom. If they didn't win in the Supreme Court, they

would never win. There would be no appeal. But if they did win, no one could ever take their freedom away from them.

Surely Roswell Field also saw a larger issue at stake, one that had been a part of many freedom suits in St. Louis. "The question," he told another lawyer, "is the much-vexed one of whether

Roswell Field wanted to take Dred's case to the U.S. Supreme Court, which would decide once and for all whether Dred was a slave or a free man.

the removal by the master of his slave to Illinois or Wisconsin works [causes] an absolute emancipation [freedom]." At first, however, *Dred Scott v. Sanford* was about family more than anything else. One family—that of Irene Sanford Emerson Chaffee and her brother John—wanted to hold on to its slave property. The other family, the Scotts, wanted their freedom. As the case made its way through the courts, it became clear that Dred and Harriet Scott also wanted to be treated as human beings. They wanted to be considered citizens of the United States with certain basic rights.

As a first step, Dred and Harriet and their daughters filed suit in U.S. Circuit Court in St. Louis in November 1853. They claimed that John Sanford of New York was holding them illegally as slaves. While their suit was being considered, Dred and Harriet Scott lived in a kind of limbo. They were still slaves, and the sheriff was still collecting their hiring-out fees. But Dred listed himself in the St. Louis city directory for 1854 and 1855, something slaves did not do. He and Harriet were living in a hut or lean-to in an alley between Tenth and Eleventh Streets downtown, just north of Washington Street. Dred was working as a whitewasher. Harriet took in laundry. The girls were kept away someplace safe. Together, Dred and Harriet worked and waited.

In May 1854, their suit came before the federal court in St. Louis. In Missouri, popular opinion in support of slavery was enough to outweigh years and years of law that said Dred was free. Dred lost the case, but his lawyer wasn't discouraged. Field hadn't really expected to win in St. Louis. He was hoping against hope, and maybe even against good sense, to win in Washington, D.C. He was hoping to convince a majority of the judges on the U.S. Supreme Court to agree with what Dred Scott had been saying all along: "That he was & is a free man . . . unjustly & unlawfully held in Slavery."

CHAPTER SIX

The Dred Scott Decision

V ERY RARELY IN HISTORY, A SMALL STORY ABOUT A few ordinary people and their hopes and dreams becomes a big story about a nation and all its hopes and dreams. That's what happened with Dred and Harriet Scott's Supreme Court case. It was called *Scott v. Sandford*. (A clerk misspelled John Sanford's last name, and the mistake has been in the official record ever since.) The first arguments began in February 1856.

In the nearly two years since the Scotts had lost their case in Missouri, Roswell Field and others had been busy working on Dred and Harriet's behalf. Someone, perhaps Field or his assistant Arba Crane, put together a twelve-page pamphlet about Dred Scott and his case, published on July 4, 1854. The pamphlet told Dred's story, putting it in quotation marks so it seemed as if Dred were talking to the reader.

"To my fellow-men," Dred began, "I lay before you the record of a suit which I have brought to get the freedom of myself, my wife and children." The pamphlet set out the question covered in Dred's previous cases. If a slave was taken by his master to a place where slavery wasn't legal, was he free? And did he remain free if he returned to a slave state? The Missouri Supreme Court had decided that even if Dred were free in Illinois or at

Fort Snelling, his right to be free disappeared as soon as he returned to Missouri.

"I thought it hard," said Dred of that decision, "that white men should draw a line of their own on the face of the earth and on one side of which a black man was to become no man at all. . . ."

Dred ended by asking for help. "My fellow-men," he said, "can any of you help me in my day of trial? Will nobody speak for me at Washington, even without other hope of reward than the blessings of a poor black man and his family. I do not know. I can only pray that some good heart will be moved to pity to do that for me which I cannot do for myself; and that if the right is on my side it may be so declared by the high court to which I have appealed."

Roswell Field was a good enough lawyer to argue in front of the Missouri Supreme Court, but Dred Scott needed a more experienced lawyer if he were to stand a chance of winning in Washington. Field and the Scotts needed to find someone to speak for Dred in Washington, someone who might do so for free. By Christmastime 1854, the pamphlet hadn't produced any offers from lawyers interested in arguing the case. Roswell Field was beginning to lose hope. But he took time away from his family on Christmas Eve to write a letter to Montgomery Blair.

Blair was a Washington, D.C., lawyer with St. Louis roots. He had served as mayor of the city before moving to the nation's capital in 1852. (After his death, his Washington mansion, Blair House, would become the vice president's residence.) Blair was just the kind of lawyer the Scotts needed. He understood

Montgomery Blair agreed to argue Dred's case before the U.S. Supreme Court. He had
to be a persuasive speaker because no witnesses could be called to the stand.

southern views about slavery. He was tall and commanded one's
attention. His voice may have been a bit high pitched, but he was
known for making sound arguments in court.

Blair took the job, and starting on February 11, 1856, he presented Dred Scott's case to the U.S. Supreme Court in Washington,
D.C. Two lawyers working for John Sanford argued the other
side. The Scotts weren't present. No one there seemed to remem-
ber that *Scott v. Sandford* was about parents seeking freedom for
their daughters. Instead, Sanford's lawyers talked about whether
the old law Congress had made in 1820 to keep slavery out of
the territories–called the Missouri Compromise–was legal. Did
Congress really have the right to say whether slavery was legal
in territories?

For several months, the justices of the Supreme Court thought
about the arguments on each side. But they could not come to a
decision. Instead, they asked the lawyers for both sides to present
more arguments. In particular, they wanted to hear the lawyers
argue whether Dred Scott even had the right to bring a suit. They
asked, was Dred a citizen? Only citizens had the right to file suits
against residents of other states. Clearly John Sanford was a citizen of New York. Was Dred, a slave, a citizen of Missouri? For
that matter, could any slave be a citizen, who would have the
right to sue in court?

Just before Christmas 1856, lawyers for Scott and Sanford got
their chance to try to persuade the justices. Looking at the Court,
Montgomery Blair must have realized that he would not have an
easy time. The head of the Supreme Court was Chief Justice

Roger Taney, a wealthy southerner. Taney had sold his slaves when he was young, but he always supported slavery. By 1856, he was nearly eighty years old and sickly, or at least it seemed that way, as he constantly fussed about his health. He was tall but bent over with age. No one who looked at him thought he was all that interesting—until they heard him speak. Taney held listeners spellbound.

Including Taney, five of the justices were proslavery southerners. Two of the justices from the North were considered "doughfaces," northerners who supported slavery. Of the nine justices, only one was known to be against slavery.

The justices took their time. Months passed before they were ready to rule on the case of *Scott v. Sandford.* The weather was clear that Friday morning, March 6, 1857. Lawyers and reporters and curious citizens packed into the courtroom to hear the final decision. John Sanford wasn't there. In just a few weeks, he would die in an insane asylum. Dred and Harriet and Lizzie and Eliza weren't there either. But their future was. It rested in the hands of Chief Justice Taney.

At around eleven o'clock, Taney and the other justices came into the low, ground-level room. All were dressed in their usual black robes. All were quiet, except Taney. With a voice that grew slowly weaker, the chief justice read the majority's decision.

Reporters scribbled in their notebooks. In those days, there were no tape recorders to capture Taney's words or television cameras to spread the news of the Court's decision. Instead, reporters took notes of the morning's speech to be printed in the next day's newspapers. It would be months before Justice Taney prepared his full decision and had it printed for the public to see. But no one needed to see the full decision to know that Dred and his family were still slaves.

Taney's opinion was clear from his words about American blacks: "history shows that they have, for more than a century been regarded as beings of an inferior order, and unfit associates for the white race, either socially or politically; and had no rights which white men were bound to respect; and the black man might be reduced to slavery, bought and sold, and treated as an ordinary article of merchandise."

Taney was summing up the history of blacks in America as he saw it, starting in colonial times. But many people in the courtroom thought he was stating his opinion of blacks in the 1850s. Newspaper accounts in the days that followed frequently quoted Taney as saying that blacks *have* no rights that white men need respect.

If black slaves had no rights that whites need respect, then they couldn't be citizens. They couldn't file suits as Dred had done against John Sanford. And they were bound to be forever slaves. One of Sanford's lawyers had said as much in court, when he argued that slavery would last "for all time."

When the news reached St. Louis that March, little changed for Dred and Harriet. They were still slaves. They were still hired out for wages, wages that would now be paid to John Sanford or Irene Emerson Chaffee. Eliza was eighteen and Lizzie eleven–old enough to be hired out or sold, with their parents or on their

Chief Justice Robert Taney of the U.S. Supreme Court was a long-time supporter of slavery. He and the majority of the other justices decided that Dred was not a free man.

own. Dred and Harriet would have nothing to say in the matter. After all, the U.S. Supreme Court had decided that a slave could be "treated as an ordinary article of merchandise."

Though the Court's decision did little to change the Scotts' lives, it charged like a speeding steam train through the heart of America's debate over slavery. *Scott v. Sandford* changed everything.

IN MARCH 1857, Americans read their newspapers and pondered Justice Taney's decision. There was much to consider. Taney's decision went well beyond determining whether Dred Scott should be free. The Court decided first that *no* black person living in the United States could be considered a citizen of the United States, or even a citizen of a state. Taney said that the Constitution made this clear, even though the word *slavery* is not used in the Constitution. With *Scott v. Sandford,* the rights of slaves and of all *free* blacks were in doubt. As Taney had written in an earlier court decision, "The privileges they are allowed to enjoy, are accorded to them as a matter of kindness and benevolence rather than of right."

The Court also ruled that Congress never had the right to keep slavery out of territories. Slaves, after all, were property. Congress had no right to interfere with what people did with their property. *Scott v. Sandford* said that the Missouri Compromise of 1820 forbidding slavery in territories was illegal. If that was so, then Dred and Harriet Scott had not become free by living at Fort

Snelling. Dred hadn't become free when he was taken to Illinois, either, because Taney agreed with the Missouri Supreme Court's ruling. That decision said that Missouri laws should decide Dred's status as a slave in Missouri, even if he had earlier spent time in a free state.

By getting rid of the law of 1820, *Scott v. Sandford* made it possible for slavery to spread over vast stretches of the United States–territories that would eventually be carved into a dozen states. Taney's decision made it possible, even likely, that slavery would spread and grow in ways that it could not have before.

For Americans who opposed slavery, *Scott v. Sandford* was a rallying cry. Before Dred Scott's case, slavery's opponents hadn't been very united. They hadn't come together behind a presidential candidate who opposed slavery. They hadn't flocked to a single political party that wanted to end slavery. After Dred Scott's case, antislavery forces in America became united in their fury and disgust.

America's most famous black man, the abolitionist and former slave Frederick Douglass, made a speech in May 1857 about *Scott v. Sandford*. He called it "an open, glaring, and scandalous tissue of lies" that cleared the way for "slavery [to] go in safety anywhere under the star-spangled banner." But Douglass wasn't without hope. In fact, he said, "my hopes were never brighter than now." Taney, Douglass admitted, could do many things. But, Douglass went on, "He cannot bale out the ocean . . . or pluck the silvery star of liberty from our Northern sky. . . . He cannot change the essential nature of things–making evil good, and good, evil."

Frederick Douglass, a fugitive slave, began speaking out against slavery in the 1840s.

Scott v. Sandford ended Dred and Harriet's hopes for freedom through the courts. But, said Douglass, "this very attempt to blot out forever the hopes of an enslaved people may be one necessary link in the chain of events preparatory to the downfall and complete overthrow of the whole slave system." Douglass believed that Taney's decision was just plain wrong. In order to make that wrong right, slavery had to end. Douglass predicted that there would be a "wild and deadly struggle for freedom."

Most Americans in the 1850s trusted the Supreme Court to make good and fair decisions. But to many Americans who opposed slavery, the Court's decision in *Scott v. Sandford* was so bad, so contrary to past laws, and so strange a reading of the Constitution that it didn't deserve to be enforced.

It struck an Illinois lawyer named Abraham Lincoln that way. Lincoln was a candidate for U.S. Senate in 1858. When he debated his opponent, Lincoln frequently referred to Dred Scott and to Justice Taney's decision. On June 16, he spoke of proslavery and antislavery forces in America, comparing the nation to a house whose residents were of differing opinions: "A house divided against itself cannot stand," Lincoln said. "I believe this government cannot endure, permanently half slave and half free. . . . Either the opponents of slavery will arrest the further spread of it . . . or its advocates will push it forward till it shall become alike lawful in all the States—old as well as new, North as well as South."

Lincoln did not win election to the U.S. Senate, but he later became a candidate for president. He ran as a member of the Republican Party, a party whose purpose in part was to end slavery in

Abraham Lincoln, pictured here with son Tad, signed the
Emancipation Proclamation during the Civil War in 1863, freeing slaves
in areas rebelling against the Union.

the United States. Soon after Lincoln was elected president in 1860, the nation became divided in a civil war. Abraham Lincoln seemed to have predicted the Civil War in his speech about the "house divided." Frederick Douglass seemed to have been talking about it when he spoke of a "wild and deadly struggle for freedom." Chief Justice Taney may even have hoped to prevent it by ruling once and for all on slavery in 1857.

The Civil War raged between 1861 and 1865. Not long after the war's end, Americans approved two amendments to the U.S. Constitution. These amendments began to change the way blacks were treated in America. The Thirteenth Amendment ends slavery, saying that "Neither slavery nor involuntary servitude, except as punishment for crime whereof the party shall have been duly convicted, shall exist within the United States, or any place subject to their jurisdiction." The Fourteenth Amendment, ratified in 1868, guarantees blacks the rights of citizens.

These two amendments brought freedom and the promise of dignity to countless slaves, but not to the Scotts. Their freedom came shortly after Justice Taney read the Court's decision in 1857. But it didn't come the way anyone expected.

Taylor Blow, the son of Dred's original owner, signed freedom bonds for Dred and Harriet Scott, freeing them and daughters Eliza and Lizzie.

CHAPTER SEVEN

Free at Last

T HE TREES NEAR THE COURTHOUSE IN ST. LOUIS
were already in leaf on May 26, 1857. That's when all the paper-
work was in order. That's when Taylor Blow, now a man of nearly
forty years, signed freedom papers for Dred Scott and his family.
Taylor was one of "them boys" Dred was raised with, and he had
stuck with the family's former slave during all the years of the
freedom suit. In the end, the Scotts' freedom didn't come from
the courts. It came from a very embarrassed Irene Emerson,
now known as Irene Chaffee.

The former Mrs. Emerson had remarried, and her husband
was a Yankee and an abolitionist to boot. No one knows if she
told her new husband that she still owned a family of slaves back
in Missouri. But when her brother John Sanford died on May 5,
newspapers out East broke the story that Mrs. Calvin Chaffee of
Springfield, Massachusetts, owned Dred Scott.

Calvin Chaffee had been elected to Congress as an antislavery
candidate. It simply wouldn't do for him to own a slave, in Missouri or anywhere else. "I regard Slavery as a sin against God
and a crime against man," he told a newspaper that March. After
some prodding, and the promise that she could collect her slaves'
wages, Mrs. Chaffee agreed to transfer ownership of the Scotts to

Taylor Blow. (She couldn't free them herself without going to Missouri. So Taylor Blow did it for her–and for Dred–that day in May.)

A newspaper at the time estimated that Dred would have garnered "about $350" on the slave market. But his freedom and that of his wife and daughters was surely priceless. The family's freedom suit had lasted nearly eleven years, costing them sweat and tears and hundreds of dollars besides. Dred said it had given him a "heap o trouble," but it was worth all that trouble to have his family together and free.

Roswell Field probably helped Dred Scott find his first job as a free man. Dred worked as a porter at the Barnum Hotel where Field was boarding. He also picked up and delivered laundry for Harriet Scott. Harriet quickly built up a thriving business with help from her husband and her daughters. Dred and Harriet and Lizzie and Eliza lived in a house united. Theirs was a small place in an alley behind Carr Street, but it was home.

That June, a reporter from *Frank Leslie's Illustrated Newspaper* (the *Time* magazine of its day) interviewed Dred Scott and his wife. The Dred Scott Decision had made the Scotts famous. A white man had offered to pay a thousand dollars a month (a fortune then) if Dred would travel through the North and talk about his experiences as a slave. But Dred and Harriet had always been hard workers, and talking wasn't work. Harriet wouldn't even consider the offer. She had, she said, "always [been] able to yarn [earn] her own livin, thank God, and yarn an honest one, and she didn't want money got in dat [that] way. . . ." The Scotts would stay in St. Louis, doing honest work in the alley off Carr Street and at the Barnum Hotel.

Many visitors to the hotel where Dred worked asked for him by name. Depending on their views about slavery, they saw it as either a joke or an honor that Dred Scott carried their bags to their room. People throughout the United States were hungry to know more about the man behind the court case. The reporter from *Leslie's* was just one of several visitors to the alley off Carr Street that spring and summer.

"We found the place with difficulty," the reporter wrote, "the streets in Dred's neighborhood being more clearly defined in the plan of the city than on the mother earth." As he neared the Scotts' house, he saw "a smart, tidy-looking negress, perhaps thirty years of age, who, with two female assistants was busy ironing." (Harriet was closer to forty years old, but the rest of the description fit her well.)

When the reporter asked if this was Dred Scott's home, Harriet eyed him warily. She was used to protecting her family, and a strange white man, particularly one showing up unexpectedly, wasn't welcome. What did the reporter want of Dred, Harriet asked. Why didn't this fellow just leave them alone and "tend to his own business"?

But the reporter was persistent. He had already spoken once before with Dred Scott. And since that first meeting he'd gotten a letter of introduction from Arba Crane, one of Dred's lawyer friends.

The reporter insisted on meeting the man behind the Dred Scott Decision. So, before too long, Dred rose up from behind a second ironing table, where he'd been hiding. (Harriet feared that white men were going to steal her husband away from her, so she made sure Dred kept out of sight. He would not have been the first free black kidnapped by whites and sent down south to die as a slave.)

Once he saw the letter from Arba Crane, Dred was happy to talk with the reporter. He even agreed to meet the man at St. Louis's finest portrait studio, Fitzgibbon's Gallery, to have a photograph taken. Harriet didn't like the idea much. The devil was surely behind it, she said. But, if Dred was having his picture taken, she wanted hers and her daughters' taken, too. Harriet wanted them all to look their best. They couldn't possibly go right away, as the reporter urged. They would meet at Fitzgibbon's the next day, after they'd had a chance to freshen up.

Harriet came wearing a new dress and pretty earrings. The girls, too, were pressed and polished and looking their best. Dred wore a bow tie with his fine dark suit. The reporter saw it all with the eyes of a northerner, someone who expected his readers to be *opposed* to slavery and *disposed* to like the Scotts. "Dred Scott, as might be supposed," he wrote, "is quite humble but nevertheless a real hero, moving about the streets of St. Louis." Harriet was, he said, "neat, industrious, and devotedly attached to her husband and children. . . ." She was a churchgoer and a woman who would be much happier without the kind of fame her husband had gained. Still, Harriet posed for her portrait, as did Eliza and Lizzie.

FRANK LESLIE'S
ILLUSTRATED
NEWSPAPER

Entered according to Act of Congress, in the year 1857, by FRANK LESLIE, in the Clerk's Office of the District Court for the Southern District of New York. (Copyrighted June 22, 1857.)

No. 82.—VOL. IV.]   NEW YORK, SATURDAY, JUNE 27, 1857.   [PRICE 6 CENTS.

TO TOURISTS AND TRAVELLERS.

We shall be happy to receive personal narratives, of land or sea, including adventures and incidents, from every person who pleases to correspond with our paper.

We take this opportunity of returning our thanks to our numerous artistic correspondents throughout the country, for the many sketches we are constantly receiving from them of the news of the day. We trust they will spare no pains to furnish us with drawings of events as they may occur. We would also remind them that it is necessary to send all sketches, if possible, by the earliest conveyance.

VISIT TO DRED SCOTT—HIS FAMILY—INCIDENTS OF HIS LIFE—DECISION OF THE SUPREME COURT.

WHILE standing in the Fair grounds at St. Louis, and engaged in conversation with a prominent citizen of that enterprising city, he suddenly asked us if we would not like to be introduced to Dred Scott. Upon expressing a desire to be thus honored, the gentleman called to an old negro who was standing near by, and our wish was gratified. Dred made a rude obeisance to our recognition, and seemed to enjoy the notice we expended upon him. We found him on examination to be a pure-blooded African, perhaps fifty years of age, with a shrewd, intelligent, good-natured face, of rather light frame, being not more than five feet six inches high. After some general remarks we expressed a wish to get his portrait (we had made

ELIZA AND LIZZIE, CHILDREN OF DRED SCOTT.

efforts before, through correspondents, and failed), and asked him if he would not go to Fitzgibbon's gallery and

have it taken. The gentleman present explained to Dred that it was proper he should have his likeness in the "great illustrated paper of the country," overruled his many objections, which seemed to grow out of a superstitious feeling, and he promised to be at the gallery the next day. This appointment Dred did not keep. Determined not to be foiled, we sought an interview with Mr. Crane, Dred's lawyer, who promptly gave us a letter of introduction, explaining to Dred that it was to his advantage to have his picture taken to be engraved for our paper, and also directions where we could find his domicile. We found the place with difficulty, the streets in Dred's neighborhood being more clearly defined in the plan of the city than on the mother earth; we finally reached a wooden house, however, protected by a balcony that answered the description. Approaching the door, we saw a smart, tidy-looking negress, perhaps thirty years of age, who, with two female assistants, was busy ironing. To our question, "Is this where Dred Scott lives?" we received, rather hesitatingly, the answer, "Yes." Upon our asking if he was home, she said,

"What white man arter dad nigger fox?—why don't white man 'tend to his own business, and let dat nigger 'lone? Some of dese days dey'll steal dat nigger—dat are a fact."

DRED SCOTT. PHOTOGRAPHED BY FITZGIBBON, OF ST. LOUIS.   HIS WIFE, HARRIET. PHOTOGRAPHED BY FITZGIBBON, OF ST. LOUIS.

These sketches of Dred, Harriet, Eliza, and Lizzie Scott were made from photographs taken at Fitzgibbon's Gallery in St. Louis.

For a little more than a year, Dred and his family enjoyed their freedom together. They worked hard to pay back their legal expenses. The Scotts had spent, by their own reckoning, five hundred dollars in cash and much more in labor over the eleven years of their freedom suit. The Scotts wanted to pay it all back, and that would take time. But Dred Scott didn't have much time left. On September 17, 1858, at about age fifty-five, he died of tuberculosis.

Henry Blow offered to give Dred a proper burial, and his family agreed. Dred was buried in the St. Louis Wesleyan Cemetery. Eliza Scott died a few years later, in the middle of the Civil War. But Harriet Robinson Scott lived in St. Louis doing laundry and ironing until about 1870. She had time to savor her freedom.

The member of the family who benefited most from the long, hard struggle was Lizzie, also called Elizabeth. For a time, she lived and worked with her mother off the alley behind North Eighth Street. Later, she married Henry Madison and had seven children. Two boys–Harry and John–survived. And although Lizzie died in 1884, she passed on her memories.

She passed on memories of being hidden away and almost forgotten while living at the very center of the Dred Scott Decision. She shared memories of the harshness, uncertainty, and fear of slavery. And she passed on memories of how freedom changed so much, even if it couldn't change everything.

In 1867, the cemetery where her father was buried was abandoned. Taylor Blow paid to have Dred Scott reburied at Calvary Cemetery. He had to buy three graves, even though there was only one body. Whites didn't want to be buried next to blacks, so blacks had to buy extra spaces on either side.

In 1957, a crowd gathered by Dred Scott's grave in Calvary Cemetery. John A. Madison and Dred Scott Madison were there. A century had passed since their great-grandparents lost their final court battle, but across America blacks were carrying on the struggle for full equality in the Civil Rights movement. They were fighting for the right to be buried where they wanted, for the right to go to school where they wanted, for the right to live

Dred Scott's grave is in Calvary Cemetery in St. Louis. Taylor Blow had to buy two other burial spots, one on each side of Dred's, because few whites wanted to be buried next to a black man.

and work where they wanted. Many shared a dream of being judged, as Dr. Martin Luther King Jr. put it a few years later, not "by the color of their skin but by the content of their character."

The fight continues even now. But it started when one family dreamed of being treated as people, not property. Dred and Harriet Scott risked everything to realize that dream—to hold onto their children and make their family free.

GLOSSARY

abolitionist	one who opposes slavery
appeal	a request for a new hearing, as in a court of law
bayonet	a weapon consisting of a knife fitted to the muzzle end of a rifle
boom	to grow quickly or flourish
cat-'o-nine-tails	a whip made of nine knotted cords
cholera	a fatal disease causing dehydration
circuit court	a court that moves from one place to another within a judicial district
claim	land a settler builds on and later declares ownership of
deposition	testimony under oath; a written statement by a witness
emancipation	freedom from bondage or slavery
jumping the broom	marriage ceremony at which the bride and groom step over a broom, symbolically beginning their new lives together
justice	a judge
justice of the peace	an official with the authority to perform marriages and administer oaths
levee	a landing place on a river
panic	general alarm concerning financial matters
petition	a written request to someone in authority demanding change
plaintiff	the party that brings a case to court
quartermaster	military officer responsible for food, clothing, and equipment of troops

GLOSSARY

shoal	a sandbar or shallow place in a body of water
statement	a formal pleading, usually in a court of law
supreme court	the highest court in a state or nation
territory	a part of the United States not admitted as a state but having a governor and legislature
testimony	a declaration of truth, usually in a court of law
title	legal possession of something
tuberculosis	a disease affecting the lungs
verdict	decision reached by a judge or jury at the end of a trial
witness	one who testifies before a court

CHRONOLOGY

1787   The Northwest Ordinance prohibits slavery in American territories north and west of the Ohio River, including present-day Illinois and Minnesota.

1803   **Dred Scott** is born at about this time, presumably in Virginia, where he lives as the slave of Peter Blow.

1818   The Blow family and their slaves move to Alabama.

1820   The Missouri Compromise prohibits slavery in territories north and west of the state of Missouri.

At about this time, **Harriet Robinson** is born, probably in Virginia.

1830   The Blows, with their slaves and other possessions, move to St. Louis, Missouri, where they run the Jefferson Hotel.

1831   John Emerson, an army doctor, begins the process of purchasing the slave named Dred from Peter Blow.

1833   In November, Dr. Emerson takes Dred to his new posting: Fort Armstrong at Rock Island in Illinois, a free state.

1835   At about this time, Harriet Robinson moves with her master, Major Lawrence Taliaferro, to Fort Snelling in Wisconsin Territory, where slavery is illegal.

1836   *Rachael v. Walker* is decided in a Missouri court, with the slave Rachael gaining her freedom after her master takes her to territories where slavery is illegal.

In May, Dr. Emerson is transferred to Fort Snelling, and Dred moves there with him.

1836 or 1837   Dred Scott marries Harriet Robinson in a civil ceremony at Fort Snelling.

1838   Dr. Emerson moves with his slaves to Fort Jesup in Louisiana, but he is soon reassigned to Fort Snelling. During the return trip north, Harriet gives birth to **Eliza** in free territory.

CHRONOLOGY

1843 Dr. Emerson dies on December 29. His widow and baby daughter inherit his slaves.

1846 **Lizzie,** the Scotts' second daughter, is born at Jefferson Barracks in Missouri, a slave state. On April 6, Dred and Harriet file suit to gain their freedom.

1847 On June 30, the Scotts' first trial begins. The Scotts lose in St. Louis Circuit Court on a technicality, and their lawyer calls for a new trial.

1850 The retrial begins on January 12. The St. Louis Circuit Court declares the Scotts to be free, but Mrs. Emerson's lawyers appeal on February 13.

1852 In *Scott v. Emerson,* decided in March, the Missouri Supreme Court rules against Dred's freedom.

1854 On May 15, Dred's case comes before the federal court in St. Louis. Dred loses, but he appeals to the U.S. Supreme Court.

1856 On February 11, arguments begin in the case of *Scott v. Sandford.*

1857 On March 6, the U.S. Supreme Court rules that the ban on slavery in the territories is unconstitutional and that Dred is still a slave.

Mrs. Chaffee, formerly Mrs. Emerson, transfers ownership of the Scotts to Taylor Blow, who frees them on May 26.

1858 On September 17, Dred dies of tuberculosis at about age fifty-five.

1863 Eliza Scott dies at about this time.

1865 The Thirteenth Amendment to the U.S. Constitution abolishes slavery.

1870 Harriet Scott is believed to have died.

1884 At about this time, Lizzie Scott Madison dies in St. Louis.

NOTES

For full bibliographic citations, see the bibliography on pages 95–100.

3   "them boys he was raised with": "Visit to Dred Scott," 50.

6   "broad fields alive with slaves . . .": William Nivison Blow, n.p.

9   "there has not been a single instance . . .": Daniel S. Dupre, 41.

10 "Every time we look back . . .": Joan Cashin, 51.

10 "returnless distance": Cashin, 55.

10 "They are astonishingly large . . .": Anne Newport Royall, 114.

14 "It is not uncommon to see . . .": Royall, 227.

20 "How much is offered for this woman? . . .": William W. Brown, 707.

21 "teaching the slave that he must never . . .": William W. Brown, 707.

22 Historians disagree about how and when Dred was sold to Dr. Emerson. Most early historians assumed that Dred was sold after Peter Blow's death in June 1832. They noted that a slave named Sam, sold for five hundred dollars, was part of the inventory of Blow's possessions after his death and assumed that Sam must have been Dred's name prior to his sale to Dr. Emerson. However, Dred appears in records in Huntsville, Ala., as one of Peter Blow's slaves, as does a slave named Sam. Also, in statements to the court, both Dred Scott and Henry Blow say that Peter Blow sold Dred to Emerson. Putting together those statements and a payment made by Emerson to Peter Blow's account at a store, historians now believe that Dred was sold, perhaps in installments, to Emerson between the summer of 1831 and the fall of 1833, when Dred accompanied the doctor to Fort Armstrong.

26 Although Fort Snelling was located in Wisconsin Territory in 1836, by 1838 it was part of the newly formed Iowa Territory. This

change made for some confusion in court documents when Dred and Harriet later filed suit for freedom. In their first court documents, Dred and Harriet state that they were taken as slaves to Fort Snelling in Iowa Territory, but an agreed statement of facts for a later trial and other sources refer to the Scotts being taken as slaves to Wisconsin.

27 "At St. Louis, the last of our necessary purchases . . .": Colonel John H. Bliss, 336.

27 "Weather very unpleasant . . .": Journal of Lawrence Taliaferro, 10 May 1836.

27 "splendidly equipt with beautiful head dress . . .": Journal of Lawrence Taliaferro, 12 June 1836.

28 "[F]ew know how closely drawn together . . .": Mrs. Charlotte O. Van Cleve, 105.

30 Historians disagree over whether Taliaferro sold or gave Harriet to Emerson. According to Harriet's statements to the court, she was sold by Taliaferro to Emerson. But years later, Taliaferro made a confusing statement: "There being no minister in the country, [I] officiated as a justice of the peace, and united . . . Dred Scott with Harriet Robinson—my servant girl, which I gave him" (Lawrence Taliaferro, 235). Did Taliaferro give away his slave as his words might imply? By the time he wrote this, Taliaferro had moved to the North, had become a supporter of the Union, and had freed his slaves. Perhaps his statement reflects his wish to save face before his northern friends and neighbors. Taliaferro, in 1837, had bought and sold many slaves. He knew the value of a slave, particularly at a frontier fort where hired help was hard to come by, so it is unlikely that he would have given away such valuable property. Thomas Shaw, historian at Historic Fort Snelling, suggests that, because Taliaferro was about to leave on a long trip to the East, he wished to unload his slave property. Selling Harriet—and marrying her to Dred—might have been a practical solution to that problem (Interview, Thomas Shaw, 17 July 2002).

38 "young and likely": R. Douglas Hurt, 261.

38 "up to three hundred and fifty": The values of young slaves varied widely, according to health and other factors. In records of slave auctions from the 1820s, sales as high as $351 are recorded for girls (correspondence with Bob Moore, historian, Jefferson National Expansion Memorial, St. Louis, Mo., 31 July 2003).

42 "an eminent citizen of St. Louis . . .": "Visit to Dred Scott," 50.

42 "good man": "Visit to Dred Scott," 50.

43 "people of good standing . . .": Frederick Trevor Hill, 247.

43 "entitled to his freedom": Circuit Court Case Files, Dred Scott.

44 "Harriet, a woman of color": Circuit Court Case Files, Harriet, a woman of color.

51 "universally known there . . .": Circuit Court Case Files, Catherine Anderson.

51 "was claimed by Doctor Emerson . . .": Circuit Court Case Files, Miles Clark.

52 "I hired Dred & his wife . . .": Circuit Court Case Files, Samuel Russell.

53 "I did not hire out the negroes myself . . .": John D. Lawson, 228.

54 "he was & is a free man" and "prove that he was & is unjustly . . .": Circuit Court Case Files, Affidavit.

56 "The only way I know these negroes . . .": Lawson, 234.

58 "When he comes back here and asks you . . .": Jas. B. Gardenhire, 581. Lawson, 237, mistakenly cites this lawyer's brief as part of the 1850 trial.

58 "the taking and holding of the plaintiff . . .": Gardenhire, 581. Lawson, 237, mistakenly cites this lawyer's brief as part of the 1850 trial.

59 "On almost three sides the State of Missouri . . ."; "Times now are not as they were . . ."; "the overthrow and destruction of our government": Lawson, 239.

62 "The question is the much-vexed one . . .": Roswell Field to Montgomery Blair, 24 December 1854, quoted in Hill, 251.

65 "To my fellow-men . . .": Lawson, 244.

66 "I thought it hard . . ." and "My fellow-men . . .": Lawson, 244.

70 "history shows that they have . . .": Walter Ehrlich, *They Have No Rights,* 142.

70 "for all time": Don E. Fehrenbacher, 302.

72 "The privileges they are allowed to enjoy . . .": Fehrenbacher, 70.

73 "an open, glaring, and scandalous tissue of lies": Paul Finkelman, 174, 175.

75 "this very attempt to blot out forever . . .": Finkelman, 176.

75 "A house divided against itself cannot stand . . .": Henry Steele Commager, 345.

77 "Neither slavery nor involuntary servitude . . .": Tom Pendergast, et. al., 252.

79 "I regard Slavery as a sin . . .": "Dred Scott and Hon. C. C. Chaffee."

80 "about $350": Kaufman, 227.

80 "heap o trouble": "Visit to Dred Scott," 50.

80 "always [been] able to yarn . . .": "Visit to Dred Scott," 50.

81 "We found the place with difficulty . . .": "Visit to Dred Scott," 49.

81 "tend to his own business": "Visit to Dred Scott," 49.

82 "Dred Scott, as might be supposed . . .": "Visit to Dred Scott," 50.

86 "by the color of their skin . . .": William Safire, ed., 499.

BIBLIOGRAPHY

Books

Blow, William Nivison. *Tower Hill before the Rebellion: A History of the Small Virginia Plantation before the Civil War.* Slightly edited and computer processed by John Matthiessen Blow. Fort Lauderdale, Fla.: John Matthiessen Blow, 1991. <http://home.earthlink.net/~blowstandard/TowerHill.pdf>

Brown, John. *Slave Life in Georgia.* Savannah, Ga.: The Beehive Foundation, Library of Georgia, 1991.

Brown, William W. "Narrative of William W. Brown, a Fugitive Slave." In *I Was Born a Slave.* Vol. I. Edited by Yuval Taylor. Chicago: Lawrence Hill Books, 1999.

Brunson, Alfred. *A Western Pioneer: or, Incidents of the Life and Times of Rev. Alfred Brunson.* Vol. II. Cincinnati, Ohio: Hitchcock and Walden, 1879.

Cashin, Joan. *A Family Venture: Men and Women on the Southern Frontier.* New York: Oxford University Press, 1991.

Chapman, Blanche Adams, and Catherine Lindsay Knorr. *Marriage Bonds of Southampton County, Virginia, 1750–1800.* Self-published, 1948.

Commager, Henry Steele, ed. *Documents in American History.* 9th Ed. Vol. I. Englewood Cliffs, N.J.: Prentice-Hall, Inc., 1973.

Corbett, Katharine T. *In Her Place: A Guide to St. Louis Women's History.* St. Louis, Mo.: Missouri Historical Society Press, 1999.

Delaney, Lucy A. *From the Darkness Cometh the Light, or Struggles for Freedom.* St. Louis, Mo.: J. T. Smith, 189?.

Dupre, Daniel S. *Transforming the Cotton Frontier: Madison County, Alabama, 1800–1840.* Baton Rouge, La.: Louisiana State University Press, 1997.

Ehrlich, Walter. *They Have No Rights: Dred Scott's Struggle for Freedom.* Westport, Conn.: Greenwood Press, 1979.

BIBLIOGRAPHY

Fehrenbacher, Don E. *The Dred Scott Case*. New York: Oxford University Press, 1978.

Finkelman, Paul. *Dred Scott v. Sandford: A Brief History with Documents*. Boston: Bedford Books, 1997.

Gardenhire, Jas. B. *"Dred Scott v. Emerson." Missouri Reports*. Vol. 15. Jefferson City, Mo.: James Lusk, 1852 (576–92).

Greene, Lorenzo, Gary R. Kremer, and Antonio F. Holland. *Missouri's Black Heritage*. Columbia, Mo.: University of Missouri Press, 1993.

Hall, Stephen P. *Fort Snelling, Colossus of the Wilderness*. St. Paul, Minn.: Minnesota Historical Society Press, 1987.

Hansen, Marcus L. *Old Fort Snelling, 1819–1858*. 1918. Reprint, Minneapolis, Minn.: Ross & Haines, Inc., 1958.

Hurt, R. Douglas. *Agriculture and Slavery in Missouri's Little Dixie*. Columbia, Mo.: University of Missouri Press, 1992.

Kaufman, Kenneth C. *Dred Scott's Advocate: A Biography of Roswell M. Field*. Columbia, Mo.: University of Missouri Press, 1996.

Lawson, John D., ed. "The Trial of the Action of Dred Scott." In *American State Trials*. Vol. 13. St. Louis, Mo.: Thomas Law Book Company, 1921.

Parramore, Thomas C. *Southampton County, Virginia*. Charlottesville, Va.: University Press of Virginia, 1978.

Pearson, Thomas A. *Free Men and Women of Color in St. Louis, 1821–1860*. St. Louis, Mo.: n.p., n.d.

Pendergast, Tom, Sara Pendergast, and John Sousanis. *Constitutional Amendments: From Freedom of Speech to Flag Burning*. Vol. 2. Detroit: Gale Publishers, 2001.

Primm, James Neal. *Lion of the Valley: St. Louis, Missouri*. Boulder, Colo.: Pruett Publishing Company, 1981.

Royall, Anne Newport. *Letters from Alabama, 1817–1822*. Edited by Lucille Griffith. University, Ala.: University of Alabama Press, 1969.

Safire, William, ed. *Lend Me Your Ears: Great Speeches in History*. New York: W. W. Norton & Company, 1992.

Shipley, Alberta D., and David O. Shipley. *The History of Black Baptists in Missouri*. Kansas City, Mo.: National Baptist Convention, 1976.

Trexler, Harrison A. *Slavery in Missouri, 1804–1865*. Baltimore, Md.: The Johns Hopkins Press, 1914.

Journal Articles

Bellamy, Donnie D. "Free Blacks in Antebellum Missouri, 1820–1860." *Missouri Historical Review* 67 (1973): 198–226.

Bliss, Colonel John H. "Reminiscences of Fort Snelling." *Collections of the Minnesota Historical Society* 6 (1894): 335–53.

Bryan, John A. "The Blow Family and Their Slave Dred Scott." Parts 1 and 2. *Missouri Historical Society Bulletin* 4.4 (July/August 1948): 223–31; 5.1 (October 1948): 19–33.

Dixon, Minneola. "Dred Scott." *Oakwood Magazine* (Spring/Summer 1994): 20.

Ehrlich, Walter. "Dred Scott in History." *Westward* 1.1 (198?): 5–10.

Frazier, Thomas, and Tom Carney. "A Man Named Sam." *Adventist Heritage* 17.1 (March 1996): 53–55.

Hess, Jeffrey A. "Dred Scott: From Fort Snelling to Freedom." *Historic Fort Snelling Chronicles* 2 (1975).

Hill, Frederick Trevor. "Decisive Battles of the Law." *Harper's Monthly Magazine* 115, no. 686 (July 1907): 244–53.

Lionberger, Isaac H., and Stella M. Drumm. "Cholera Epidemics in St. Louis." *Missouri Historical Society: Glimpses of the Past* 3 (1963): 45–76.

McDonald, William Lindsey. "A Renowned Slave in the Early Life of Florence." *Journal of Muscle Shoals History* (Tennessee Valley Historical Society) 12 (1980).

Richter, Tom. "If Walls Could Talk: A Courtroom's Story." *Westward* 1.1 (198?): 2–4.

Shapiro, Norman M. "A Man Named Sam, A Boy Named Dred." *Valley Leaves* (March 1989): 143–46.

Snyder, Charles E. "John Emerson, Owner of Dred Scott." *Annals of Iowa* 21.6 (October 1938): 441–61.

Taliaferro, Lawrence. "Auto-Biography of Maj. Lawrence Taliaferro." *Collections of the Minnesota Historical Society* 6 (1894): 189–256.

Van Cleve, Mrs. Charlotte O. "A Coincidence." *Collections of the Minnesota Historical Society* 3 (1880): 103–6.

VanderVelde, Lea, and Sandhya Subramanian. "Mrs. Dred Scott." *Yale Law Journal* 106.4 (January 1997): 1033–1123.

BIBLIOGRAPHY

Newspaper Articles

"Board Erects Marker Honoring Scott." *Florence (Ala.) Times Daily*, 25 February 2001, pp. 1B, 6B.

"Death of Peter Blow, Esq." *St. Louis Missouri Republican*, 22 July 1866, p. 2.

"Dred Scott." *St. Louis Globe-Democrat*, 10 January 1886, p. 19.

"Dred Scott and Hon. C. C. Chaffee." *New York Tribune*, 17 March 1857, p. 5.

"Dred Scott Case Celebrated Here." *St. Louis Post Dispatch*, 3 March 1957, n.p.

"Dred Scott Decision Centennial Observed." *St. Louis Globe-Democrat*, 7 March 1957, p. 3A.

"Granite Marker Placed at Grave of Dred Scott." *St. Louis Post Dispatch*, 25 July 1957, p. 3B.

"Headstone Is Placed at Grave of Dred Scott." *St. Louis Globe-Democrat*, 25 July 1957, p. 7A.

"Historical Address of Hon. Wm. B. Wood, July 4, 1876." *The Florence (Ala.) Gazette*, 16 August 1876, n.p.

"The Most Famous Negro in American History Was a 'Town Character' in St. Louis." *St. Louis Globe-Democrat*, 3 July 1927, p. 6 (magazine section).

"Opinion of Chief Justice Taney." *St. Louis Missouri Republican*, 27 May 1857, p. 1; 28 May 1857, p. 1.

"The Original Dred Scott." *Washington Daily Union*, 11 April 1857, p. 2.

"Visit to Dred Scott." *Frank Leslie's Illustrated Newspaper*, 27 June 1857, pp. 49–50.

Interviews

Kenny, Thomas. Telephone conversation with genealogical researcher, Huntsville, Ala., 31 May 2001 and 8 June 2001.

Shaw, Thomas. Telephone conversation with historian, Historic Fort Snelling, St. Paul, Minn., 9 April 2002 and 17 July 2002.

Manuscript Sources

Circuit Court Case Files, Office of the Circuit Clerk. City of St. Louis, Missouri. Affidavit for new trial, 24 July 1847.

BIBLIOGRAPHY

——. Catherine Anderson. Deposition, 10 May 1847.

——. Miles Clark. Deposition, 13 May 1847.

——. Harriet, a woman of color. Petition to sue for freedom, 6 April 1846.

——. Samuel Russell. Statement, 2 June 1847.

——. Dred Scott. Petition to sue for freedom, 6 April 1846.

Minnesota Historical Society, St. Paul, Minn. 1836 Wisconsin Territorial Census Listing.

——. Nathan S. Jarvis Papers.

——. Journals of Lawrence Taliaferro, Lawrence Taliaferro Papers.

Missouri Historical Society, St. Louis, Mo. ALS Julia Webster Blow to Mary Louise Dalton, 13 March 1907. Dred Scott Papers.

——. ALS Mary Louise Dalton to Frederick Trevor Hill, 13 March 1907. Dred Scott Papers.

——. Notes of conversation with Mrs. William T. Blow [Julia Webster] by Mary Louise Dalton, 18 February 1907.

Probate Court, Saint Louis County, Va. Estate of Peter Blow, filed February term, 1834, Probate Court File No. 976.

Recorder's Office, Lauderdale County, Ala. Bond from Peter Blow to A. H. Wood, 19 February 1824, Deed Book 2, p. 148; Deed from Cypress Land Co. to Peter Blow, 28 February 1827, Deed Book 4, p. 47; Deed from P. Andrews to Peter Blow, 24 March 1827, Deed Book 4, pp. 160–61; Deed from Peter Blow to Mary Lucinda Pope, 16 February 1831, Deed Book 5, pp. 149–50.

Recorder's Office, Madison County, Ala. Peter Blow from U.S. Land Office, 5 January 1811, Certificate #1029, Tract Book No. 1, p. 34; Deed from Peter Blow to J. N. S. Jones, 3 February 1821, Deed Book G, pp. 163–65; Deed of Trust from Peter Blow to Beverly Hughes, 14 April 1821, Deed Book G, pp. 328–30; Deed from Peter Blow to James Camp, 7 December 1821, Deed Book H, pp. 79–80.

Recorder's Office, Southampton County, Courtland, Va. Will of Richard Blow, 19 December 1785, Will Book 4, pp. 179–80.

State Historical Society of Wisconsin. United States Census, 1810 Federal Census, Southampton County, Va.

——. United States Census, Federal Census, Middle Ward, City of St. Louis, Mo.

Websites

"The Dred Scott Case." St. Louis, Mo.: Washington University Libraries. http://www.library.wustl.edu/vlib/dredscott/
> This project makes accessible online all early court documents (both photographs of the originals located in the Office of the St. Louis Circuit Clerk and transcriptions) relating to Dred and Harriet Scott's suits for freedom.

"Minnesota Historic Sites: Historic Fort Snelling." St. Paul, Minn.: Minnesota Historical Society. http://www.mnhs.org/places/sites/hfs/
> This website offers a virtual tour, maps, and information about tours of Historic Fort Snelling, where costumed guides give visitors a taste of life in a frontier fort in the 1820s.

"St. Louis Historic Old Courthouse." St. Louis, Mo.: National Park Service, Jefferson National Expansion Memorial. http://www.nps.gov/jeff/och.htm
> This website allows visitors to take a virtual tour of the historic St. Louis, Missouri, courthouse, where Dred and Harriet's early trials took place. Site visitors can also listen to a fictional narrative by an actress portraying Harriet Scott.

Secession Era Editorials Project. "The Dred Scott Case (1857)." Greenville, S.C.: History Department, Furman University. http://history.furman.edu/~benson/docs/dsmenu.htm
> This project gives readers access to a variety of newspaper editorials written in reaction to the Dred Scott Decision in 1857.

INDEX

INDEX

PICTURE CREDITS